AF441772

THE MIRROR OF 5THS/4THS

DECODING THE CIRCLE AFTER 300 PLUS YEARS

BY THOMAS NGANDA MUIGAI

ISBN 978-9914-708-70-7

Ordering information: For details contact tnmuigai1973@gmail.com

First edition 2021

ISBN 978-9914-708-70-7 (Paperback)

Acknowledgment: Madam Margaret Wamoro Muigai for prayers, physical, material and spiritual support.

A catalogue version is available at Kenya National Library Services

DEDICATION

To all persons who will get hold of this book, may you find it helpful, entertaining and above all practical in your journey to learn music.

Lastly to **Margaret Wamoro Muigai** my loving mum and **Rosaline Wamoro** my daughter may the almighty keep the flame of faith burning continuously and never forget **Nakuru Dundori.**

TABLE OF CONTENTS

INTRODUCTION

●Music theory generally starts with the note C.

●This will be our beginning of learning the musical alphabet C D E F G A B and its applications in music theory.

●The first major scale to learn in music theory is C major scale.

●This is because the C major scale is the easiest to understand. It is a neutral key/scale as it has no sharps or flats in its key signature.

HOW THE MIRROR WORKS

●The mirror is divided into two sides:

1. The sharp side **(#).**

2. The flat side **(♭).**

●When using the mirror, we will move sequentially and systematically from one letter to the next either from left to right or from right to left.

●When moving from left to right we will refer to this as going up in perfect 5ths intervals which is the same as going down in perfect 4ths intervals.

●When moving from right to left we will refer to this as going down in perfect 5ths Intervals which is the same as going up in perfect 4ths intervals.

●The mirror can be used in many different ways but for now we will deal with:

1. Finding out major and minor keys.

2. Figuring out key signatures for major and minor keys and this is knowing the number of sharps or flats in any key and their order.

3. Figuring out the different types of chords and their notes.

4. Finding notes that are a whole step apart.

5. Finding notes that are a tritone apart.

●One added advantage of using the mirror is when you are dealing with enharmonic notes and keys/scales as we will see next.

●Using this book, you will learn the three distinctive methods for creating any major or minor key/scale.

1. Using the mirror as mentioned earlier.

2. Creating on paper.

3. Creating on keyboard.

ENHARMONICS

●The notes with a slash are known as **enharmonic notes** and they are the **same pitch** as each other.

●For example A# is enharmonically equivalent to B♭, they are just spelled differently on the musical staff.

●The key/scale that you are in determines the spelling of a particular note in that key/scale.

●For example if you are in the key/scale of F major then you will spell the fourth note as B♭ and not A#, if you are in the key/scale of B major than you will spell the seventh note as A# and not B♭, as we will see in chapter 5 when forming both major and minor keys/scales.

●F major key/scale: F G A **B♭** C D E F

●B major key/scale: B C# D# E F# G# **A#** B

• Enharmonics can refer to notes, keys/scales or chords which are same in pitch that is they sound the same but they bear different names and are notated differently on the musical staff.

• Enharmonic equivalent intervals are slightly different from enharmonic notes and keys/scales but follow the same principle and this is that two notes can be the same distance apart but are spelt differently.

ENHARMONICS TO NOTE ON THE MIRROR

1. ENHARMONIC NOTES

•These are notes that have two different names for example B#/C but are played with the same key on the keyboard and so they have tones or pitches that sound the same and yet they are notated or spelled differently on the musical staff.

•Other examples worthy to note on the mirror are C♭/B, F♭/E, E♭/D#, G♭/F#, D♭/C#.

2. ENHARMONIC KEYS/SCALES

•These are both major and minor keys/scales that have the same pitches or sound the same but are notated or spelled differently on the musical staff because they have different note names in their keys/scales.

•The reason for this is that we have the option of writing a scale/key using either sharps or flats only as shown on the mirror, making it easier to compose and read music since we are using only one type of accidental.

***Enharmonic keys/scales are six pairs: 3 major pairs and 3 minor pairs.**

●B major/C ♭ major, F# major/G ♭ major, C# major/D ♭ major.

●g# minor/a ♭ minor, d #minor/e ♭ minor, a# minor/b ♭ minor.

ENHARMONIC NOTES ON THE SHARP SIDE OF THE MIRROR

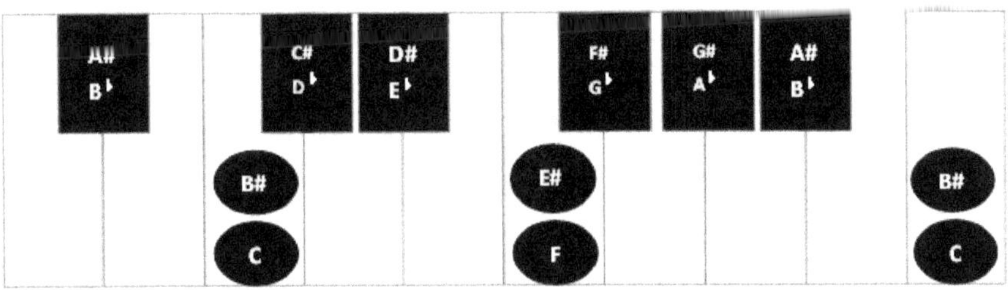

ENHARMONIC NOTES ON THE FLAT SIDE OF THE MIRROR

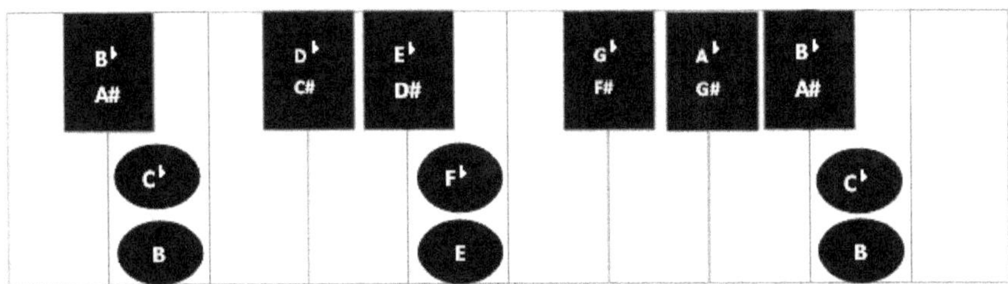

●All the black keys on the keyboard are enharmonic meaning they can either be sharp or flat and all the white keys are natural keys meaning they are not sharp or flat but technically speaking B can be called C ♭ and C can be called B#, likewise E can be called F ♭ and F can be called E#, this comes in handy when forming and naming both the major and minor scales/keys as we will see in chapter 5.

ENHARMONIC LETTERS ON THE MIRROR WORTH NOTING

1. B#/C   B# or C

•If you go up one letter to the right of these two letters you will land on G on the mirror.

•This is going up a perfect 5th interval which is equal to 7 half steps from B#/C to G on the keyboard.

•B# and C are enharmonic notes and these two letters are represented by the same note on the keyboard.

•If you go down one letter to the left of B# on the mirror you land on E# and if you go down one letter to the left of C on the mirror you land on F.

•Now E# and F are enharmonic notes and these two letters are represented by the same note on the keyboard.

•Going down one letter to the left of either B# or C is going down a perfect 5th interval which is equal to 7 half steps from B#/C to E#/F on the keyboard.

2. C♭/B   C♭ or B

•If you go down one letter to the left of these two letters you will land on F♭ and E on the mirror respectively.

•F♭ and E are enharmonic notes and these two letters are represented by the same note on the keyboard.

•Going down one letter to the left of either C♭ or B on the mirror is going down a perfect 5th interval which is equal to 7 half steps from C♭/B to F♭/E on the keyboard.

3. F ♭ /E   F ♭ or E

•If you go down one letter to the left of these two letters you will land on A on either side of the mirror along line 3.

•This is going down a perfect 5th interval which is equal to 7 half steps from F ♭ /E to A on the keyboard.

•F ♭ and E are enharmonic notes and these two letters are represented by the same white note on the keyboard.

•If you go up one letter to the right of these two letters you will land on C ♭ and B respectively.

•Now C ♭ and B are enharmonic notes and these two letters are represented by the same white note on the keyboard.

•Going up one letter to the right of either F ♭ or E on the mirror is going up a perfect 5th interval which is equal to 7 half steps from F ♭ /E to C ♭ /B on the keyboard.

LETTERS C AND A ON THE MIRROR

1. C

•If you go up one letter to the right of C either on line 2 or 3 on both sides of the mirror you will land on G.

•Going up one letter to the right of C to G on the mirror is going up a perfect 5th interval which is equal to 7 half steps from C to G on the piano or keyboard.

•If you go down one letter to the left of C either on line 2 or 3 on both sides of the mirror you will land on F.

•Going down one letter to the left of C to F on the mirror is going down a perfect 5th interval which is equal to 7 half steps from C to F on the keyboard.

2. A

•If you go up one letter to the right of A either on line 2 or 3 on both sides of the mirror that is the sharp side and the flat side you will land on E.

•Going up one letter to the right of A to E on the mirror is going up a perfect 5th interval which is equal to 7 half steps from A to E on the keyboard.

•If you go down one letter to the left of A either on the line 2 or 3 on both sides of the mirror you will land on D.

•Going down one letter to the left of A to D on the mirror is going down a perfect 5th interval which is equal to 7 half steps from A to D on the keyboard.

•**TIP:** When you are dealing with enharmonic key signatures you need to compare both keys/scales so as to find out which key/scale is easier to read and play in.

•For example if you compare C# major key/scale and D♭ major key/scale you will notice that one has fewer accidentals than the other, making it easier to read or play in the key of D♭ major key/scale which has five flats unlike its enharmonic equivalent C# major key/scale which has seven sharps.

•Same case applies for B major key/scale and its enharmonic equivalent C♭ major key/scale.

•C# major key/scale: C# D# E# F# G# A# B# C#

•D♭ major key/scale: D♭ E♭ F G♭ A♭ B♭ C D♭

LETTERS C ♭ AND A ♭ ON THE MIRROR

1. C ♭

• If you go up one letter to the right of C ♭ either on line 1 or 2 on the flat side of the mirror you will land on G ♭ .

• Going up one letter to the right of C ♭ to G ♭ on the mirror is the same as going up a perfect 5th interval which is equal to 7 half steps from C ♭ to G ♭ on the keyboard.

• Now this black note on the keyboard is an enharmonic note and it can either be called G ♭ or F#.

• But since we are on the flat side of the mirror, we will designate this note the letter G ♭ on our mirror.

• If you go down one letter to the left of C ♭ either on line 1 or 2 on the flat side of the mirror you will land on F ♭ .

• Going down one letter to the left of C ♭ to F ♭ on the mirror is the same as going down a perfect 5th interval which is equal to 7 half steps from C ♭ to F ♭ on the keyboard.

• Now this white note on the keyboard is an enharmonic note and it can either be called F ♭ or E.

• But since we are on the flat side of the mirror we will designate this note the letter F ♭ .

2. A ♭

• If you go up one letter to the right of A ♭ either on line 1, 2 or 3 on the flat side of the mirror you will land on E ♭ .

•Going up one letter to the right of A ♭ to E ♭ on the mirror is going up a perfect 5th interval which is equal to 7 half steps from A ♭ to E ♭ on the keyboard.

•Now this black note on the keyboard is an enharmonic note and it can either be called E ♭ or D#.

•But since we are on the flat side of the mirror we will designate this note the letter E ♭ on the mirror.

•If you go down one letter to the left of A ♭ either on line 1, 2 or 3 on the flat side of the mirror you will land on D ♭ .

•Going down one letter to the left of A ♭ on the mirror is going down a perfect 5th interval which is equal to 7 half steps from A ♭ to D ♭ on the keyboard.

•Now this black note on the keyboard is an enharmonic note it can either be called D ♭ or C#.

•But since we are on the flat side of the mirror we will designate this note the letter D ♭ .

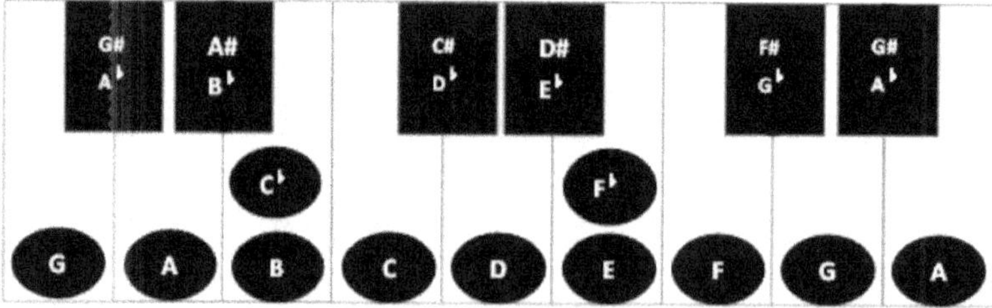

•Finally, before we begin

•We will need to differentiate between notes and the different types of chords that we will encounter.

•To do this we will do two things:

1. Notes are designated numbers 1 to 8. These are called scale degrees but for now we will refer to them as numbers.

2. Chords are designated Roman numerals I to VII and they will represent the chord whose root note is the number of the note in the major or minor scale.

●Uppercase Roman numerals will represent major chords.

●Lowercase Roman numerals will represent minor chords.

●This principle of numbering the chords with Roman numerals will apply for all our major keys but for the chords in the minor keys the Roman numerals numbering is a bit different as we will see later.

●The note numbering 1 to 8 is the same for both major and minor keys.

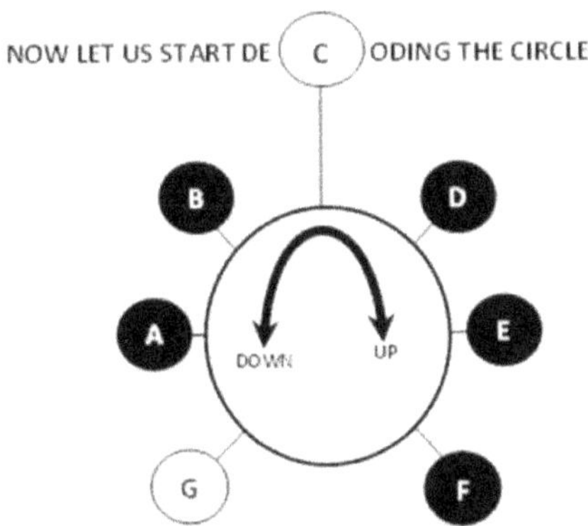

●The letters on line 1, 2 and 3 can represent either: notes, keys or chords.

RELATIONSHIP BETWEEN ANY TWO ADJACENT NOTES ON EITHER SIDE OF THE MIRROR

●**THE SHARP SIDE (#)**

1. C TO G (CDEFG): This is going up a 5th interval.

2. C TO G (CBAG): This is going down a 4th interval.

3. G TO C (GFEDC): This is going down a 5th interval.

4. G TO C (GABC): This is going up a 4th interval.

●THE FLAT SIDE (♭)

1. C TO F (CBAGF): This is going down a 5th interval.

2. C TO F (CDEF): This is going up a 4th interval.

3. F TO C (FGABC): This is going up a 5th interval.

4. F TO C (FEDC): This is going down a 4th interval.

● Let us consider relationship numbers one and four on the sharp side of the mirror and relationship numbers two and three on the flat side of the mirror to help us see how our circle is connected to the mirror of 5ths/4ths.

TIP: All the letters to the right of F on the sharp (#) side of the mirror including F itself are all sharps and all the letters to the left of B on the flat (♭) side of the mirror including B itself are all flats.

TIP: The sum of sharps (#) and flats (♭) in the key signatures of major and minor keys that are polar opposites on the mirror is always seven accidentals except for C major key and (a) minor key because they are neutral keys. For example A major key has 3 sharps therefore A ♭ major key will have 4 flats, likewise f sharp minor key has 3 sharps therefore f minor key will have 4 flats.

TIP: The accidentals (sharps and flats) along line 2 and 3 start at F# and are connected in a straight line all the way to B ♭ , all the other notes along line 2 and 3 are natural notes with no sharps or flats.

THE MIRROR OF 5THS/4THS

𝄞	0	1	2	3	4	5	6	7	7	6	5	4	3	2	1	0	𝄞
1		f#	c#	g#	d#	a#	e#	b#	fb	cb	gb	db	ab	eb	bb		1
2	C	G	D	A	E	B	F#	C#	Cb	Gb	Db	Ab	Eb	Bb	F	C	2
3	a	e	b	f#	c#	g#	d#	a#	ab	eb	bb	f	c	g	d	a	3

UNIVERSAL MNEMONIC DEVICE

1. FOR CAKES GOOD DOUGHNUTS ASK ED'S BAKERY.
2. CAKES GOOD DOUGHNUTS AT ED'S BAKERY FOR CELEBRITIES.
3. ATTENTION EVERY BIG FANCY CELEBRITY GOES DOWN AMICABLY AT ED'S BAKERY FOR CAKES GOOD DOUGHNUTS AlWAYS.

•Numbers 0-7 from left to right on the sharp side of the mirror shows the number of sharps for major and minor keys and the order in which they are arranged on the musical staff this is called the **key signature**.

•Likewise Numbers 0-7 from right to left on the flat side of the mirror shows the number of flats for major and minor keys and the order in which they are arranged on the musical staff.

•Let's take line 2 to represent major scales and line 3 minor scales.

•Let's take C major and (a) minor keys, the notes on line 1 above these two notes is the key signature for these two keys.

•C major and (a) minor keys have no sharps or flats in their key signatures on both sides of the mirror either on the sharp side or the flat side.

•Let's take E major and c# minor keys, the notes on line 1 above these two notes from left to right starting at 1 to 4 which are F#, C#, G# and D# this is the key signature in this order for this two keys when written down on the musical staff.

•Let us take C♭ major and a♭ minor keys the notes on line 1 above these two notes from right to left starting at 1 to 7 which are B♭,E♭,A♭,D♭,G♭,C♭, and F♭ this is the key signature in this order for these two keys when written down on the musical staff.

CHAPTER 1

THE SHARP (#) SIDE OF THE MIRROR FIGURING OUT THE MAJOR KEYS

- We will start with the letter C on the left side of the mirror along line 2 and move sequentially from left to right to find all our other major keys.

- This is because C will be our first major key/scale since it's a neutral key with no sharps or flats in its key signature.

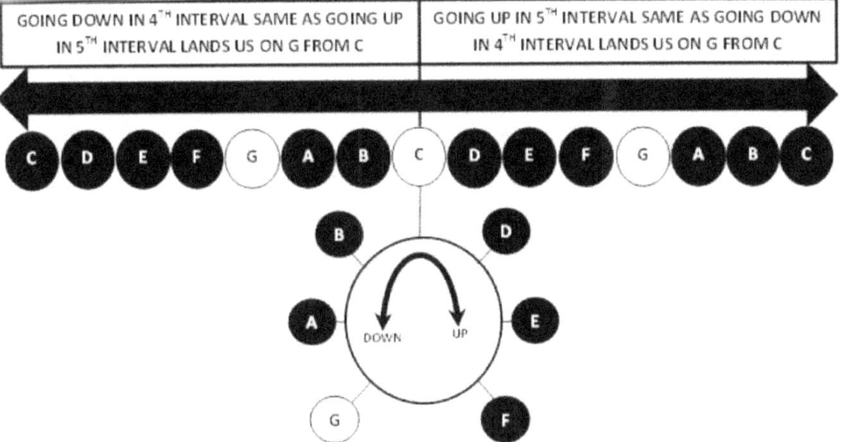

- Next we will go up one letter to the right of C and we will land on G major key on our mirror.

- This is going up a perfect 5th interval which is equal to 7 half steps from C to G on the keyboard. Inversely you can go down a perfect 4th interval which is equal to 5 half steps from C to G.

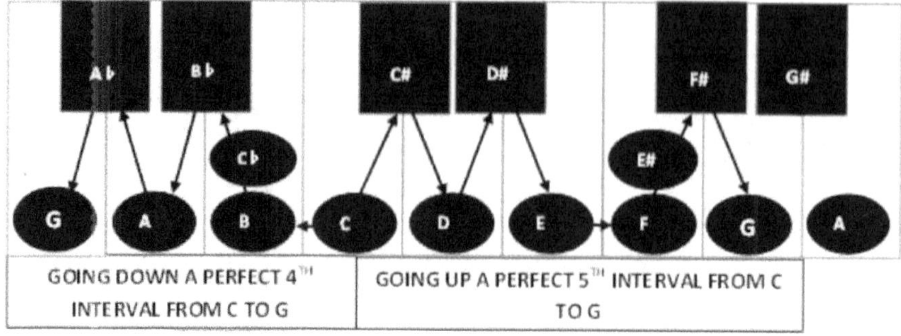

●Going up one letter to the right of G which is the same as going up a perfect 5th interval lands us on D major key. This is also the same as going down a perfect 4th interval from G to D.

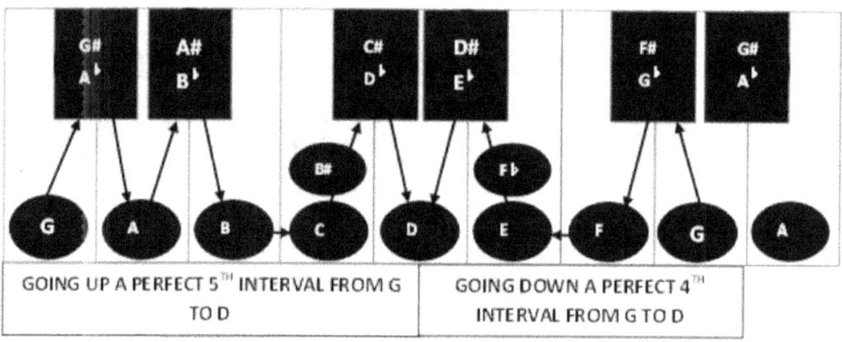

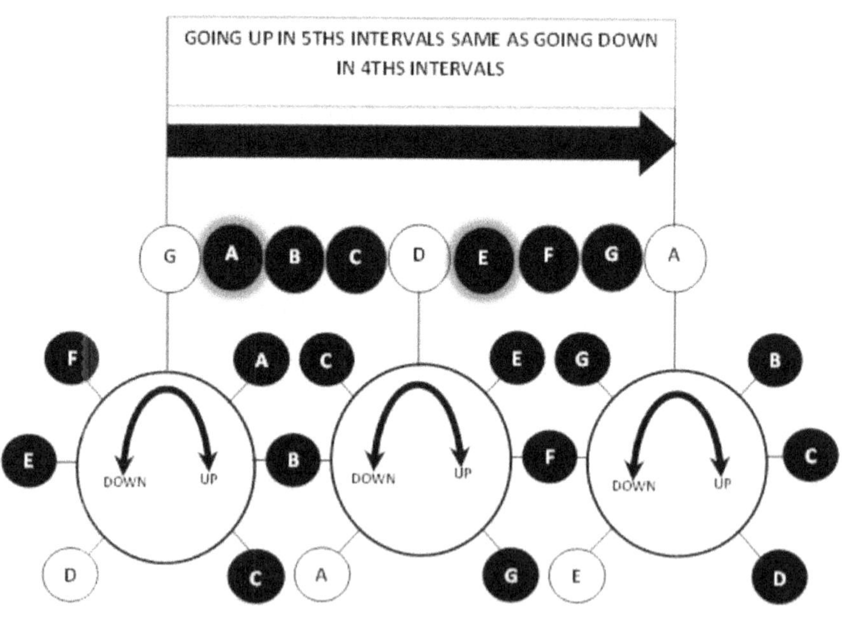

•Going up one letter to the right of D is the same as going up a perfect 5th interval landing us on A major key. This is also the same as going down a perfect 4th interval from D to A.

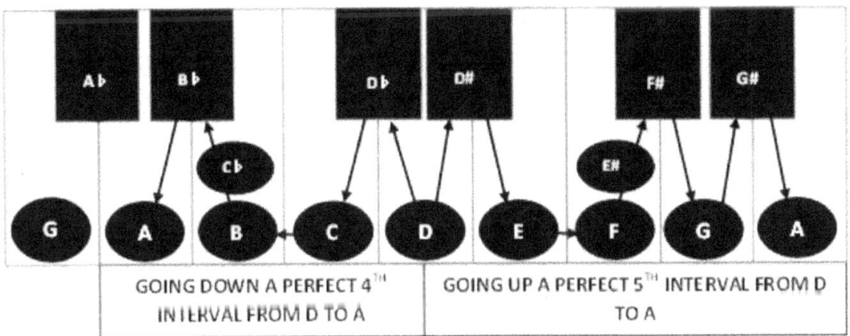

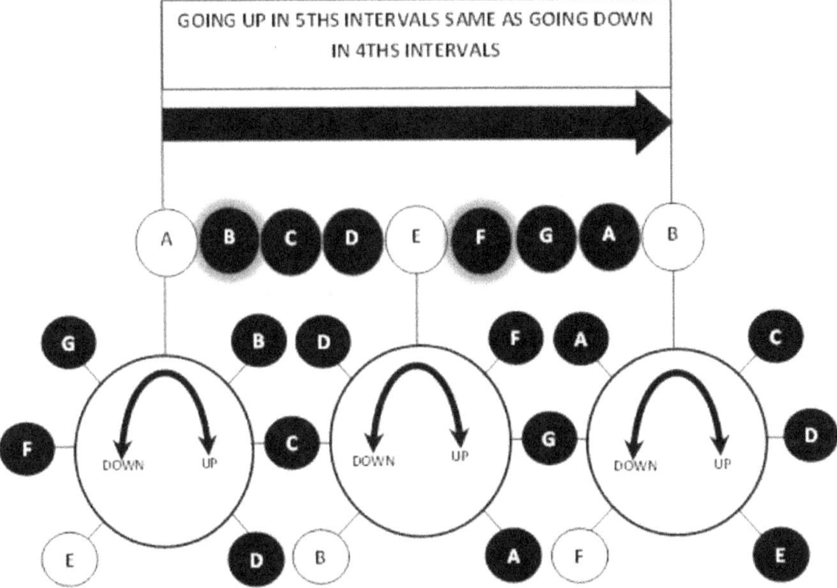

•Going up one letter to the right of A is the same as going up a perfect 5th interval landing us on E major key. This is also the same as going down a perfect 4th interval from A to E.

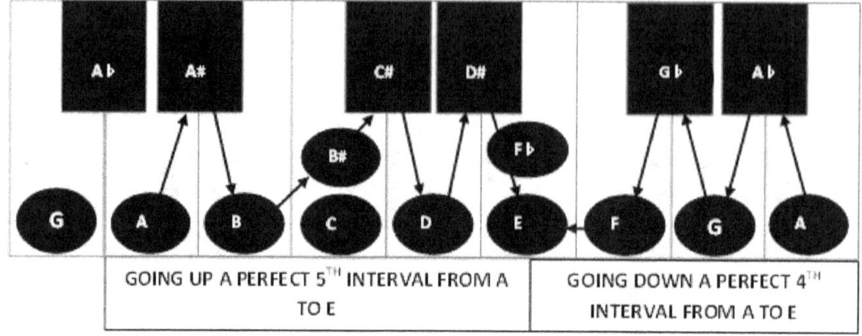

●Going up one letter to the right of E is the same as going up a perfect 5th interval landing us on B major key. This is also the same as going down a perfect 4th interval from E to B.

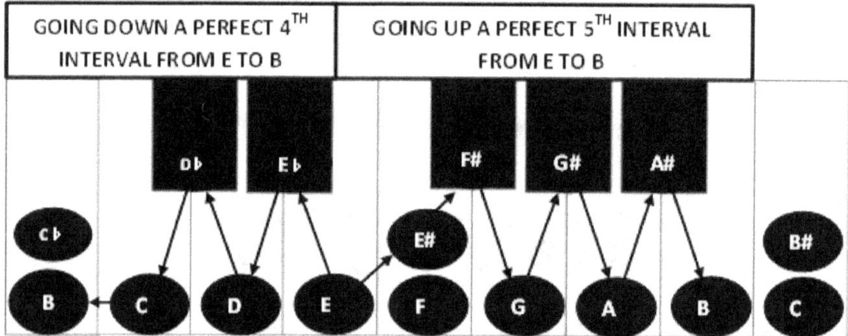

●Going up one letter to the right of B is the same as going up a perfect 5th interval landing us on F # major key. This is also the same as going down a perfect 4th interval from B to F#.

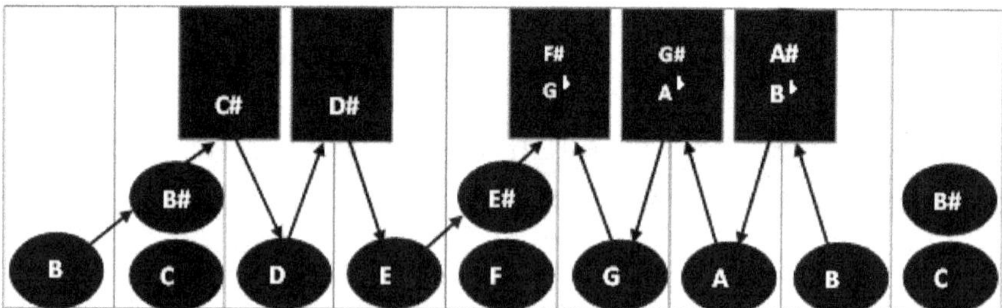

●Going up one letter to the right of B is going up a fifth interval from B to F.

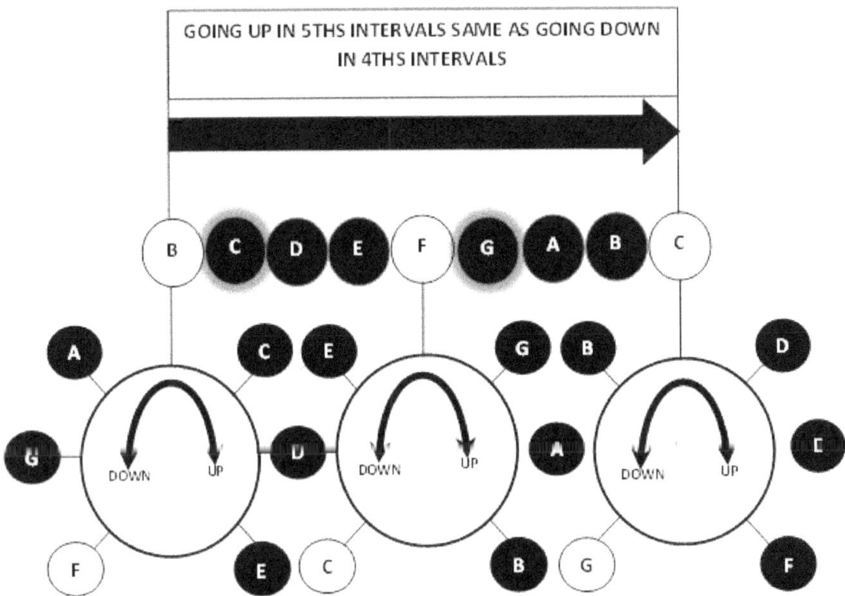

TIP: You can use your fingers to count going up or down in intervals of 5ths or going up or down in intervals of the 4ths. But for going up or down in perfect 5ths or 4ths intervals you need to count in terms of half steps.

●Going one letter to the right of the F# is the same as going up a perfect 5th interval which lands us on C # major key.

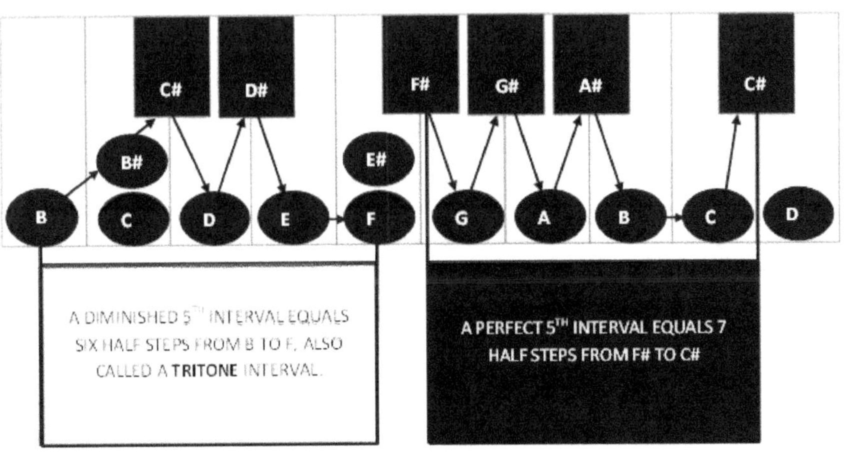

CHAPTER 2

THE SHARP (#) SIDE OF THE MIRROR FIGURING OUT THE MINOR KEYS

●Every major key has a relative minor key and every minor key has a relative major key.

●They are called relative keys because they have the same key signatures but they have different tonics or the first notes in their key or scale.

●Meaning that they share all the same notes but are arranged in different orders of whole steps and half steps as we will see later when creating major scales as well as minor scales.

●You can easily identify the major and minor keys from our mirror.

●We can take line 2 to represent major keys and line 3 to represent their relative minor keys.

●Just by looking at the mirror you can tell that if the letter on line 2 is a major key then the letter directly below it is its relative minor key for example C major and a minor, G major and e minor up to C# major and a# minor.

●If you recall at the beginning, we used C major as our neutral or starting point when figuring out all the major keys since C major key does not have any sharps or flats in its key signature.

●Now we will use a lowercase (a) as our neutral or starting point.

●We will call this note (a) minor key and it has no sharps or flats in its key signature and so will start from here and figure out all the other minor keys.

•We will start counting at (a) and move along line 3 sequentially from left to right and as you recall we will be going up in perfect 5ths intervals from letter to letter on our mirror to find all our other minor keys.

•From (a) minor key/scale for our next minor key/scale we will go up one letter to the right and we will land on e minor key/scale on our mirror.

•This is going up a perfect 5th interval which is equal to 7 half steps from A to E on the keyboard.

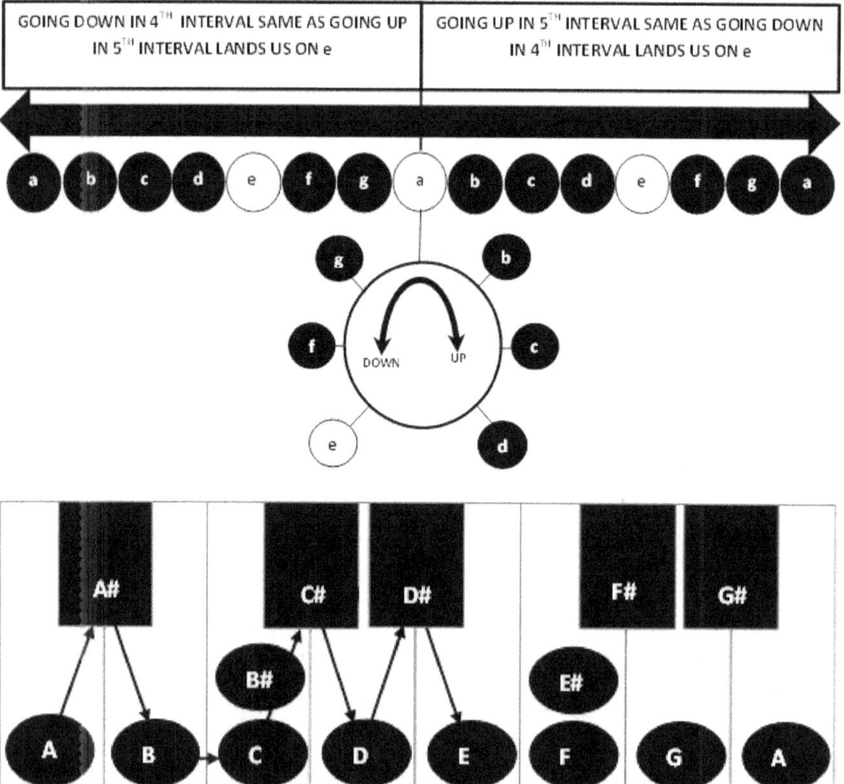

•Counting or going up a perfect 5th interval is equal to 7 half steps from A to E on the piano or keyboard.

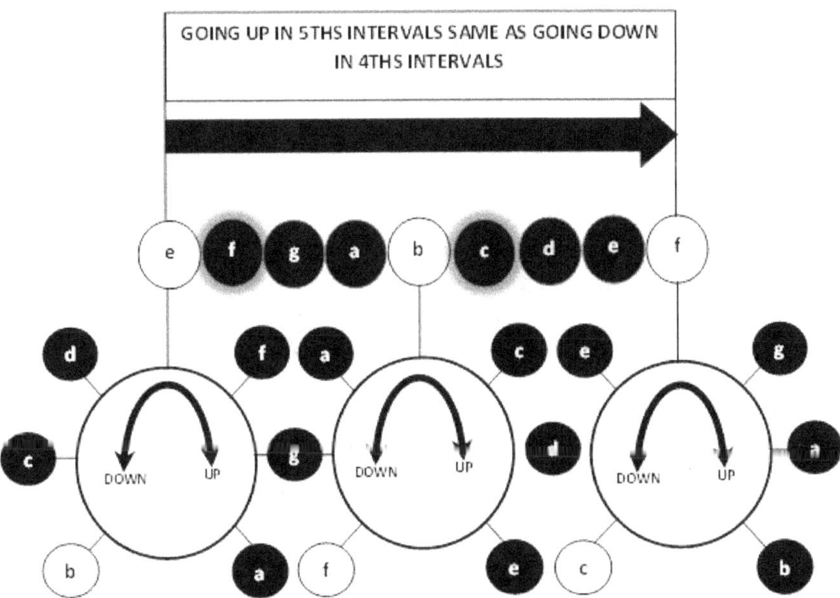

●Going up one letter to the right of e on our mirror is the same as going up a perfect 5th interval which is equal to 7 half steps on the keyboard landing us on b minor key.

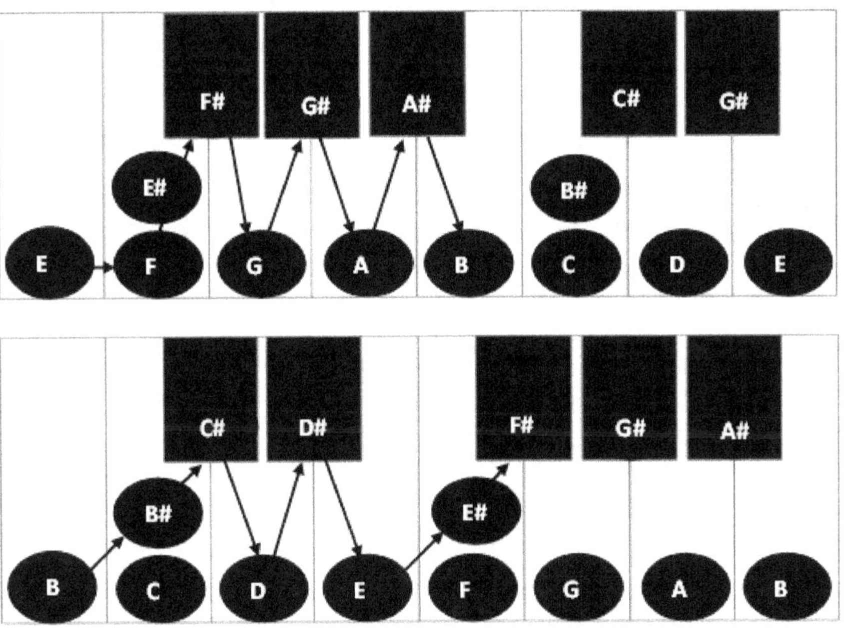

●Going up one letter to the right of b on our mirror is the same as going up a perfect 5th interval landing us on f # minor key.

●Going up one letter to the right of the f # on our mirror is the same as going up a perfect 5th interval landing us on c# minor key.

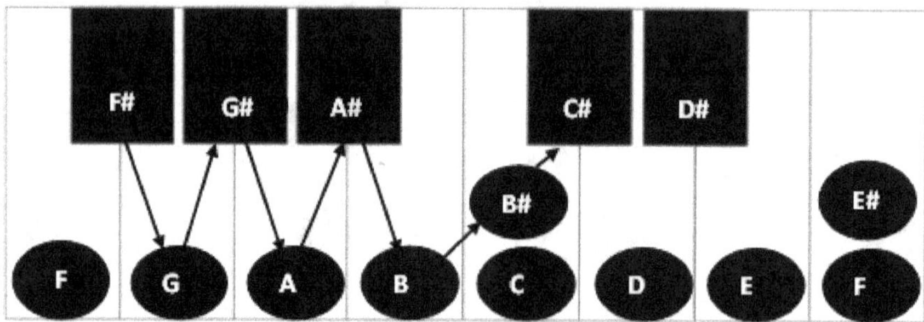

●Going up one letter to the right of c# is the same as going up a perfect 5th interval landing us on g# minor key.

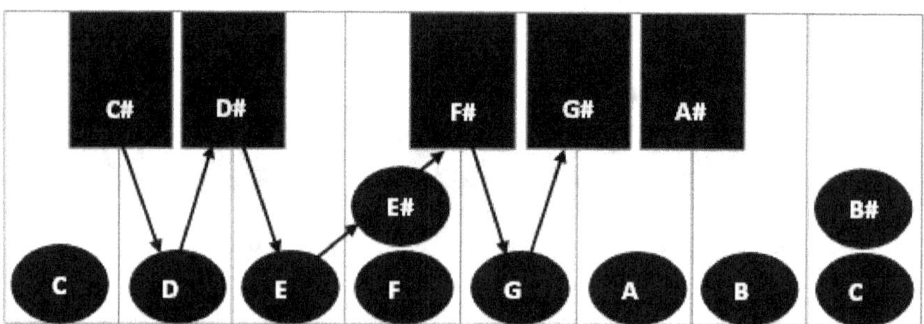

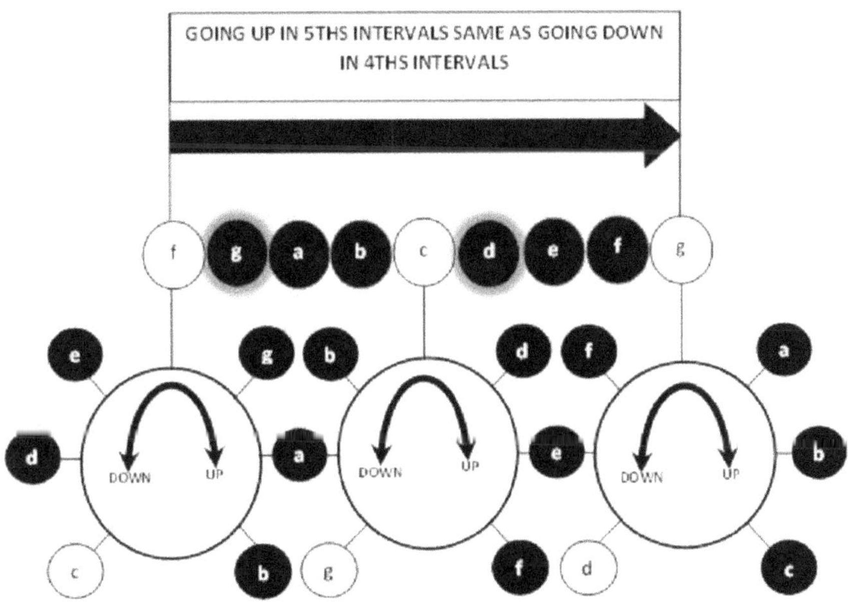

●Going up one letter to the right of g# is the same as going up a perfect 5th interval landing us on d# minor key.

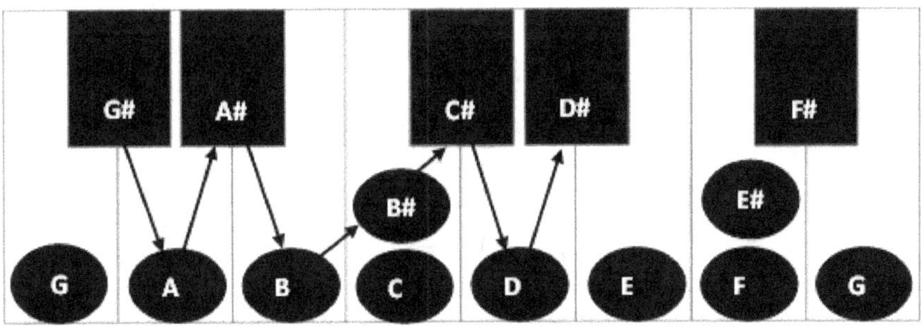

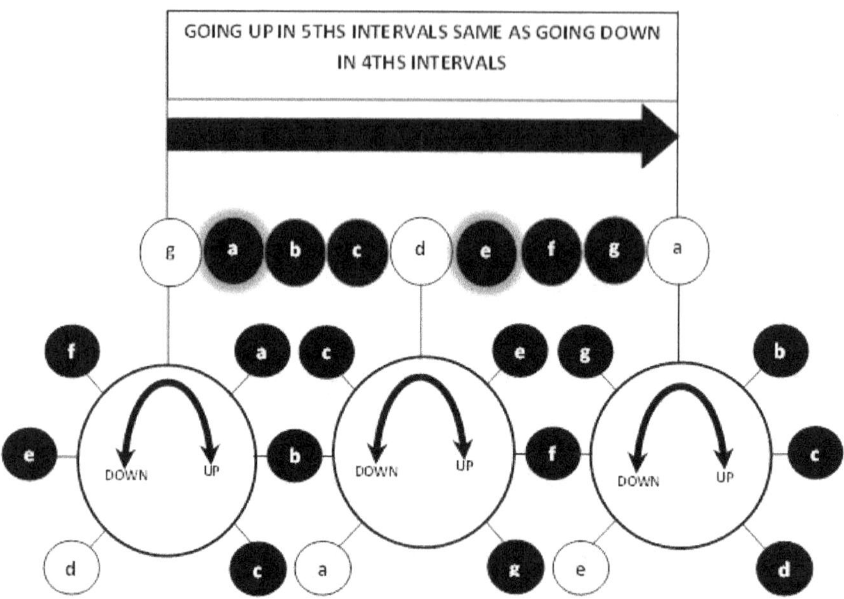

●Going up one letter to the right of the d# is the same as going up a perfect 5th interval landing us on a# minor key.

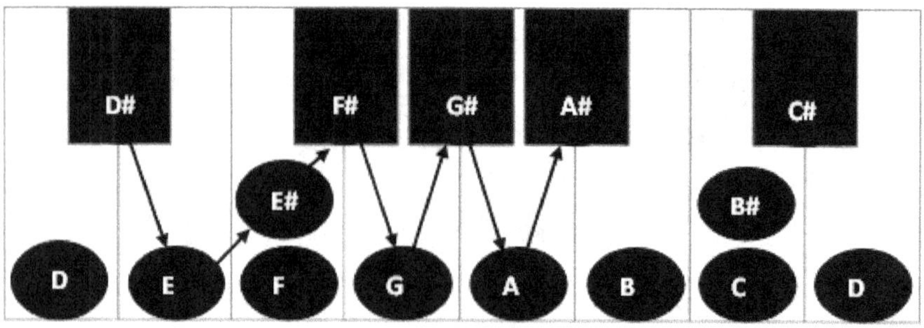

CHAPTER 3

THE FLAT (♭) SIDE FINDING MAJOR KEYS

•We will start with the letter C along line 2 on the flat side of the mirror and this time we will move sequentially from right to left to find all the other major keys on this flat (♭) side of the mirror.

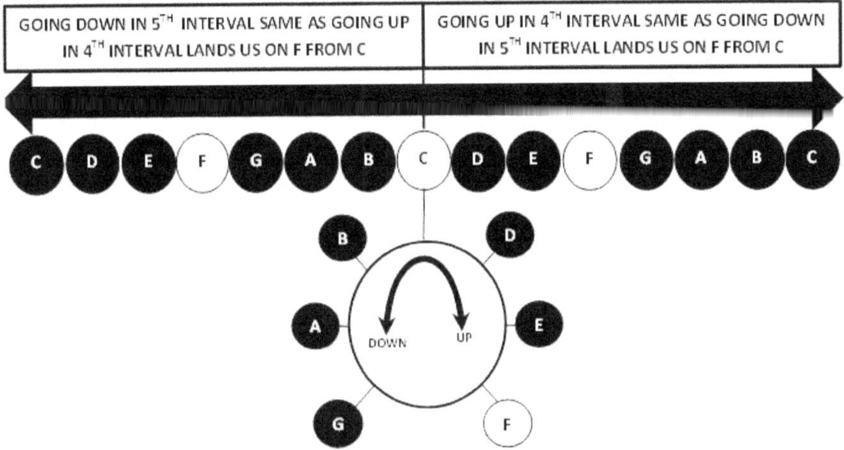

•The letter C will be our first major key and this is because the C major key is a neutral key with no sharps or flats in its key signature.

•Next, we will go down one letter to the left of C and we will land on the F major key on our mirror.

•This is going down a perfect 5th interval which is actually going down 7 half steps from C to F on the keyboard.

•Or inversely you can go up a perfect 4th interval which is equal to 5 half steps from C to C# to D to D# to E to F/E# on the keyboard.

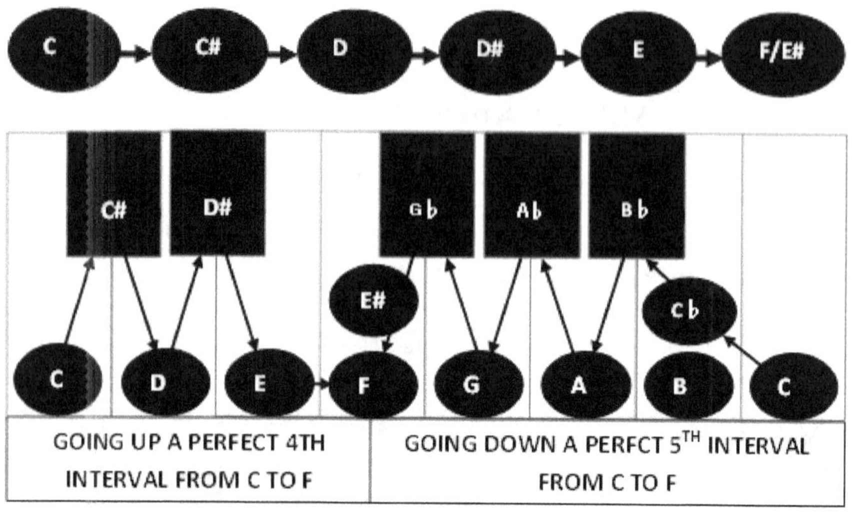

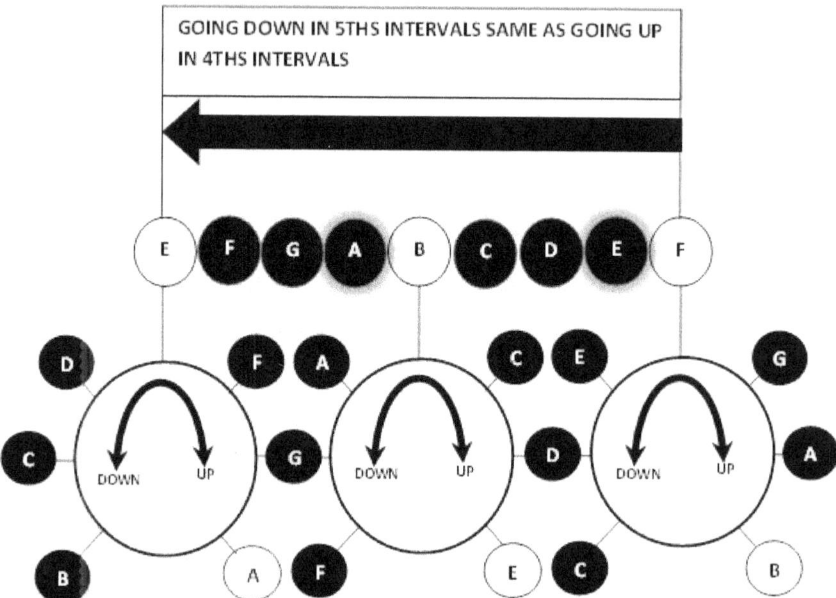

●Going down one letter to the left of F which is going down a perfect 5th interval lands us on B ♭ major key.

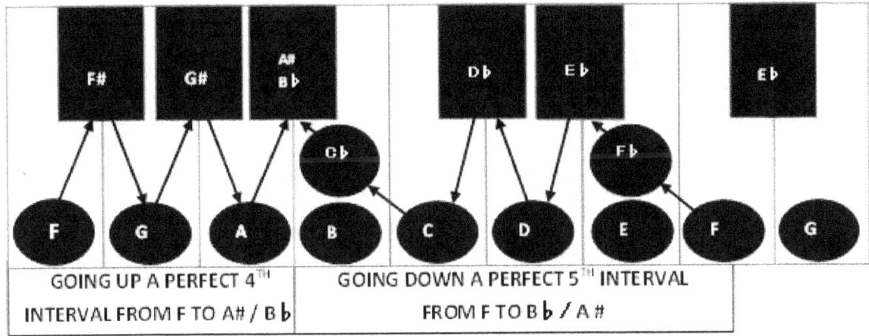

●This is the same as going up a perfect 4th interval from F to F# to G to G# to A to A#/B♭ that is:

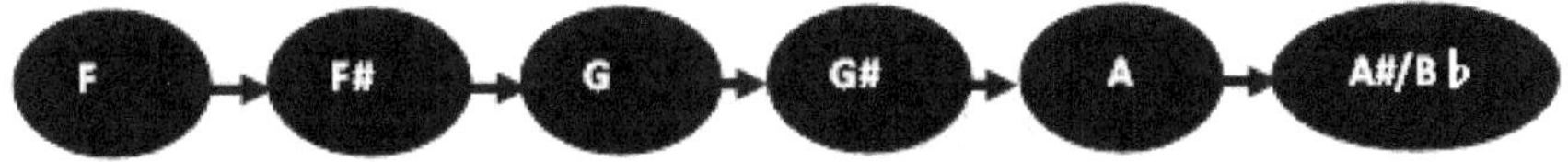

●Going down one letter to the left of B♭ is going down a perfect 5th interval which lands us on E♭ major key.

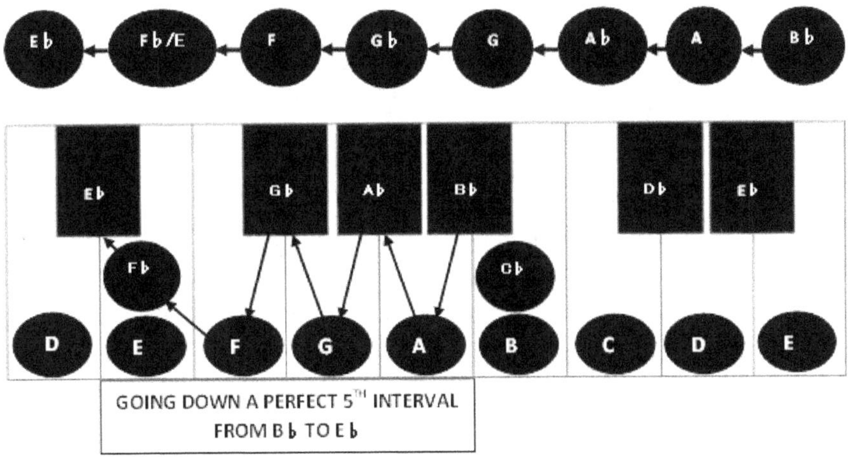

●Going down one letter to the left of E♭ is going down a perfect 5th interval which lands us on A♭ major key.

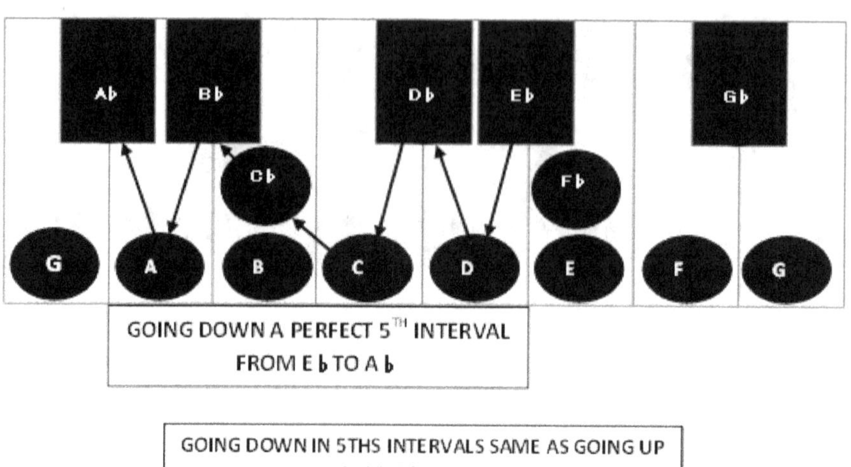

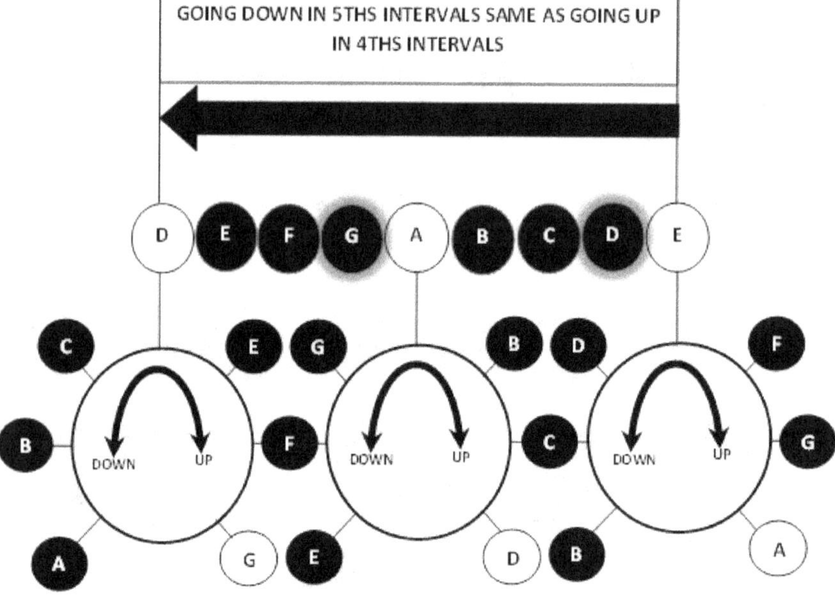

●Going down one letter to the left of A ♭ is going down a perfect 5th interval which lands us on D ♭ major key.

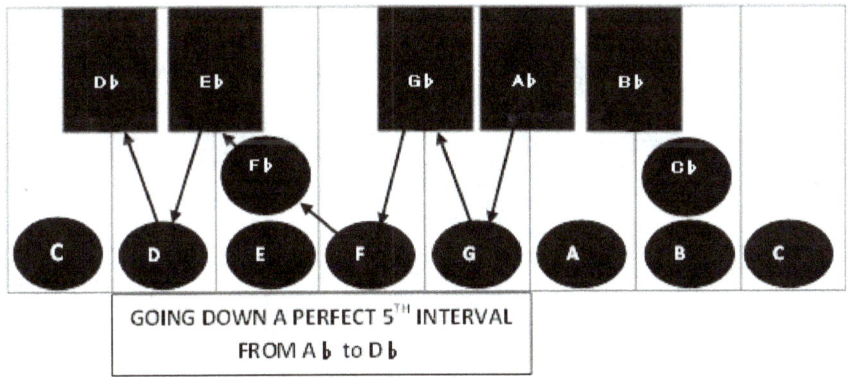

●Going down one letter to the left of D ♭ is going down a perfect 5th interval which lands us on G ♭ major key.

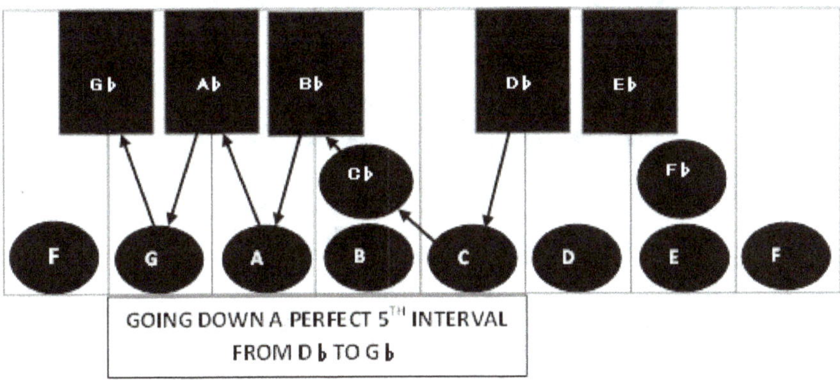

●Going down one letter to the left of G ♭ is going down a perfect 5th interval which lands us on C ♭ major key.

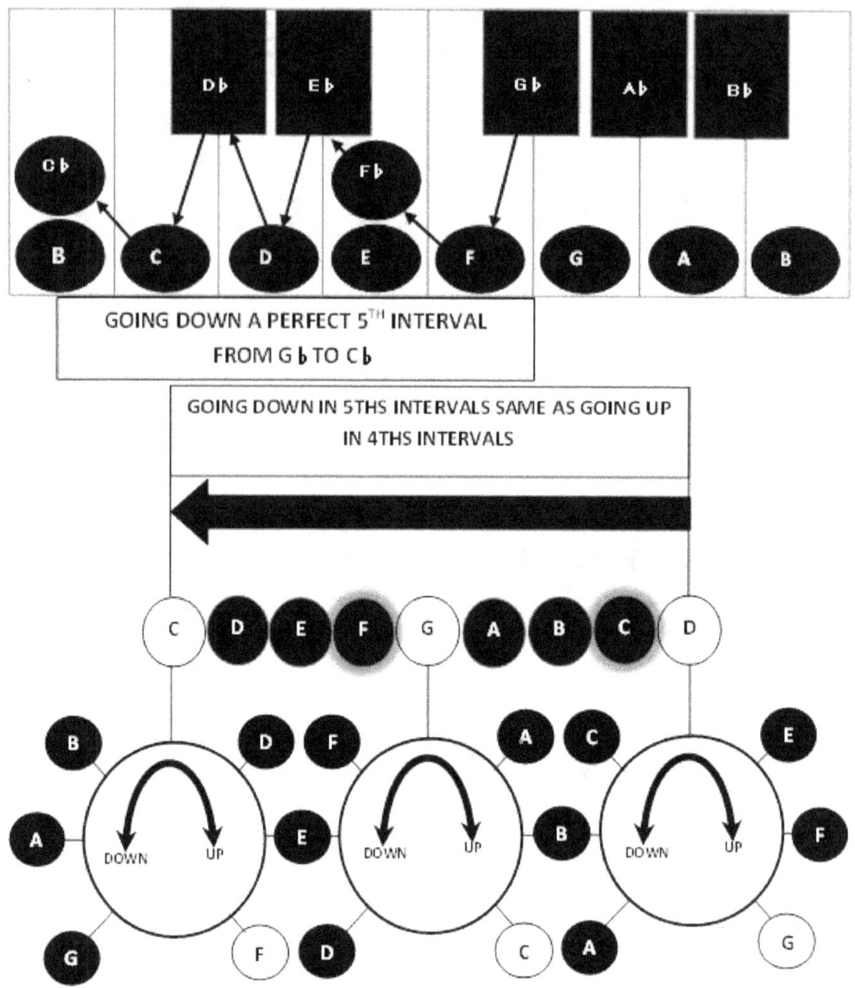

Db
Eb
Gb
Ab
Bb
Cb
Fb
B
C
D
E
F
G
A
B
GOING DOWN A PERFECT 5TH INTERVAL
FROM Gb TO Cb
GOING DOWN IN 5THS INTERVALS SAME AS GOING UP
IN 4THS INTERVALS
C
D
E
F
G
A
B
C
D
B
D
F
A
C
E
A
E
B
F
DOWN
UP
DOWN
UP
DOWN
UP
G
F
D
C
A
G

CHAPTER 4

THE FLAT (♭) SIDE FINDING MINOR KEYS

•Just by looking at the flat side of our mirror you can easily identify the major and minor keys on this side of the mirror.

•We can take line 2 to represent major keys and line 3 to represent their relative minor keys.

•Just by looking at the mirror you can tell that if the letter on line 2 is a major key then the letter directly below it is its relative minor key on line 3.

•For example, F major and d minor, B ♭ major and g minor, E ♭ major and c minor, A ♭ major and f minor, D ♭ major and b ♭ minor, G ♭ major and e ♭ minor and finally C ♭ major and a ♭ minor.

•In the same manner that we started at note C and called it our C major key which was a neutral key with no sharps or flats in its key signature.

•Likewise, its relative minor which is (a) lowercase will be our starting point.

•We will call this letter (a) minor key and being the relative minor of C major key it's also a neutral key and so it has no sharps or flats in its key signature.

•Now we will use the same principle we used when finding or figuring out our major keys on the flat side of our mirror and this is going down in perfect 5ths intervals starting at (a) and finding out all the other minor keys on the flat side of our mirror.

•We will move from right to left.

•We will start counting at (a) along line 3 and move sequentially from right to left.

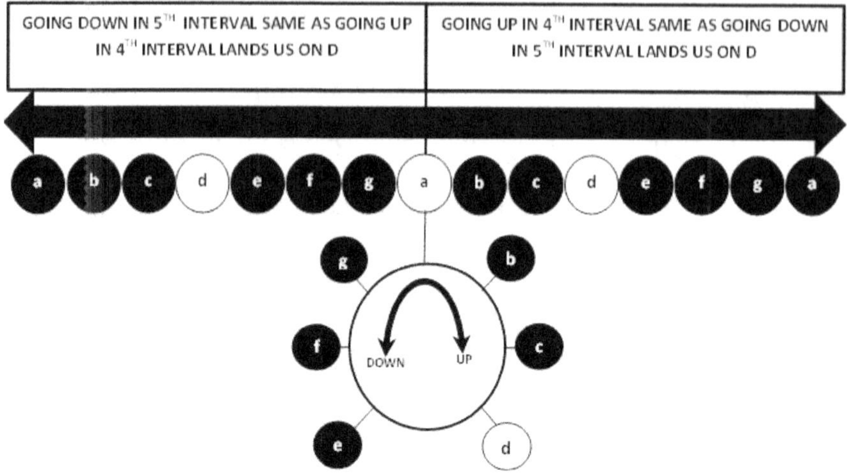

•Now we will be going down in perfect 5ths intervals from letter to letter to find all our other minor keys on the flat side of our mirror.

•We will go down one letter to the left of (a) and land on d minor key.

•This is going down a perfect 5th interval which is equal to 7 half steps from A to D on the keyboard.

•Inversely you can go up a perfect 4th interval which is equal to 5 half steps from A to A# to B to B# to C# to D.

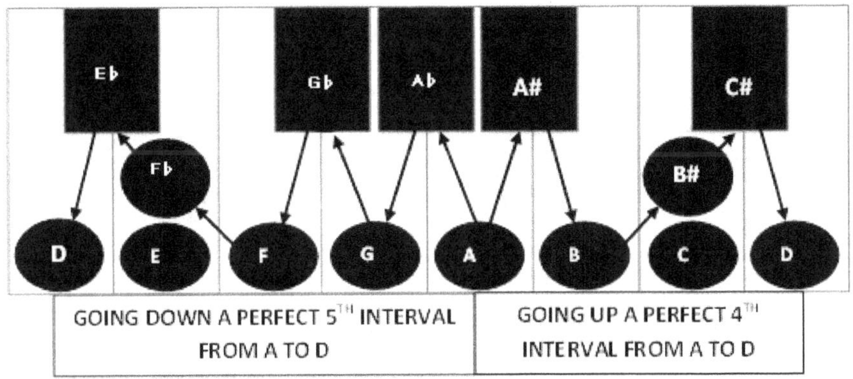

●Going down one letter to the left of d which is the same as going down a perfect 5th interval lands us on g minor key.

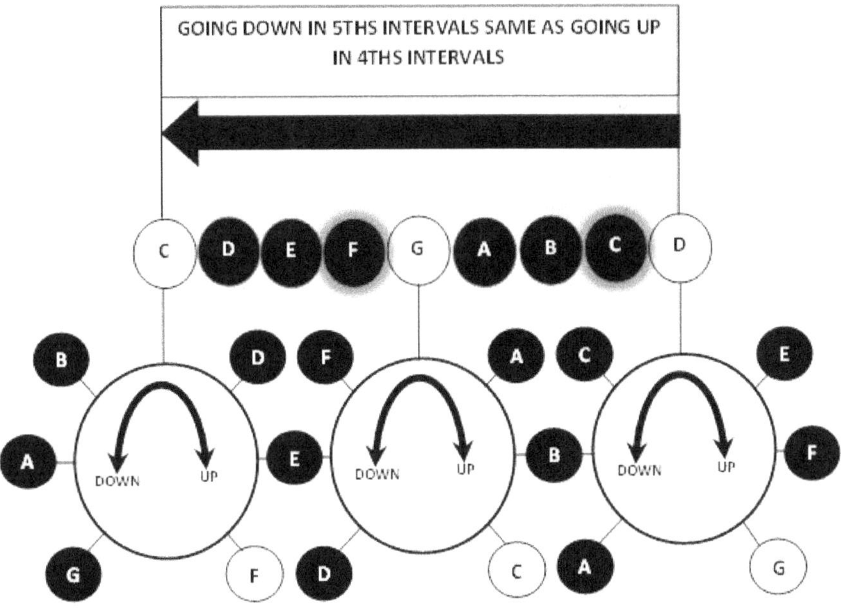

●Going down one letter to the left of d on line 3 is the same as going down a perfect 5th interval landing on g minor key.

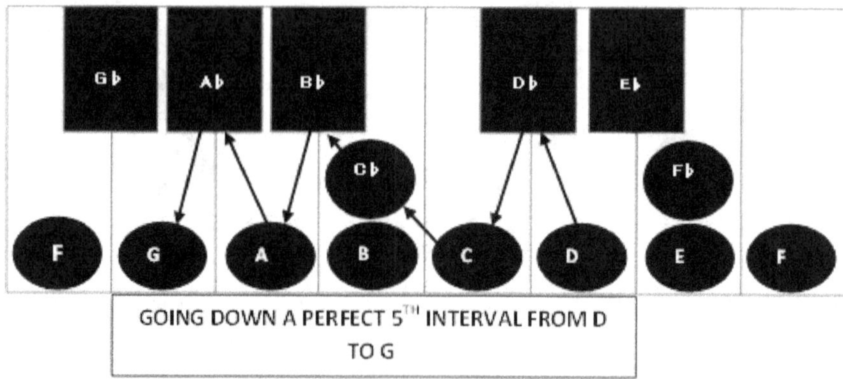

•Going down one letter to the left of g which is the same as going down a perfect 5th interval lands us on c minor key.

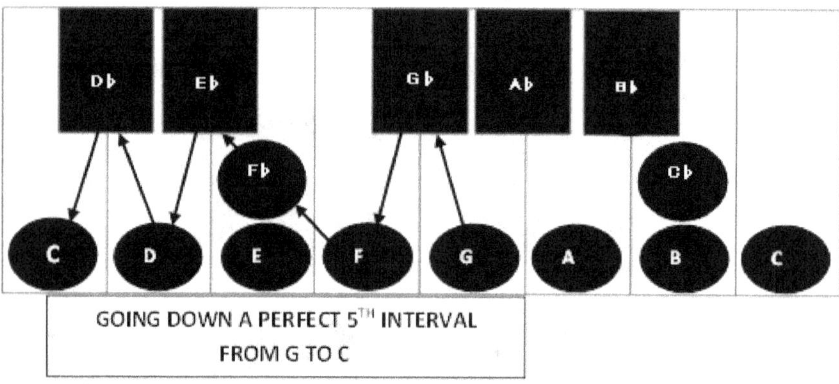

•Going down one letter to the left of c which is the same as going down a perfect 5th interval lands us on f minor key.

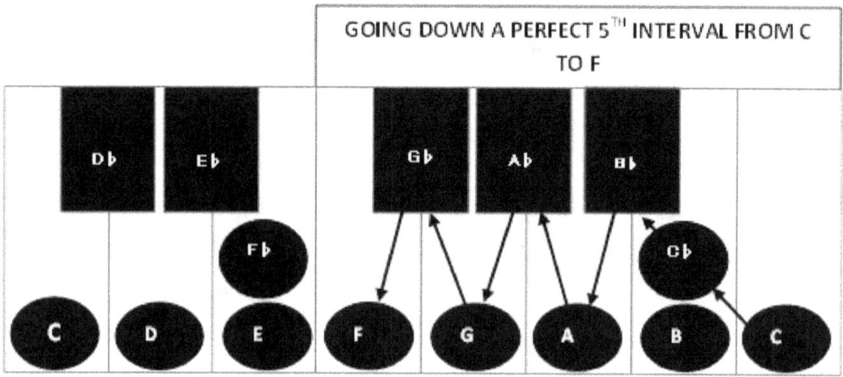

•Going down one letter to the left of f is the same as going down a perfect 5th interval landing us on b♭ minor.

•Remember now that we are going down in perfect 5ths intervals.

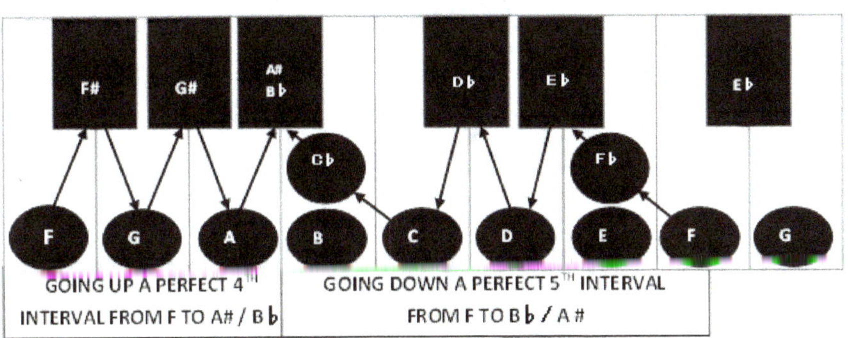

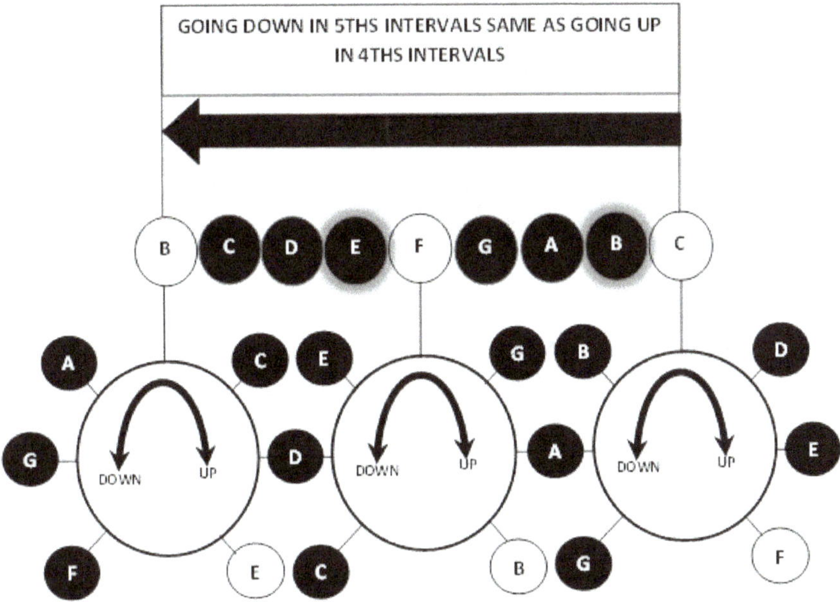

•Going down one letter to the left of b♭ is actually going down a perfect 5th interval landing us on e♭ minor key.

•This is equal to going down 7 half steps from B♭ to E♭ on the keyboard which is also the same as going up a perfect 4th interval which is equal to 5 half steps from B♭ to E♭.

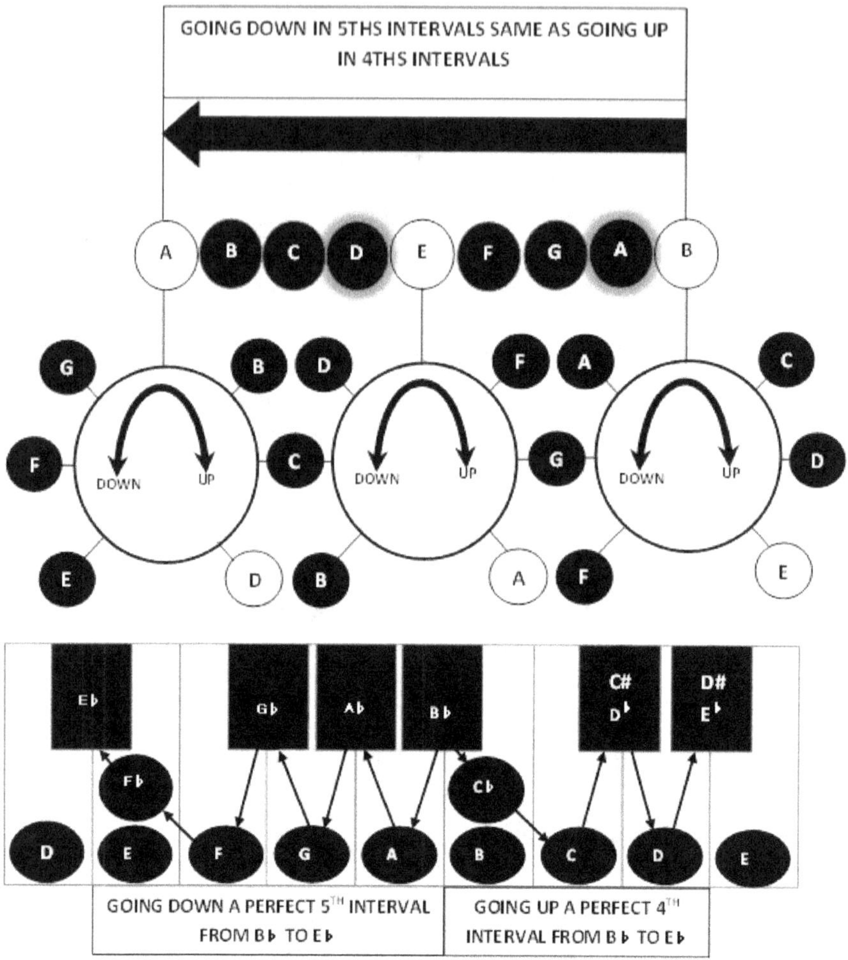

●Going down one letter to the left of e ♭ is actually as going down a perfect 5th interval landing us on a ♭ minor key.

●This is equal to going down 7 half steps from E ♭ to A ♭ on the keyboard which is also the same as going up a perfect 4th interval which is equal to 5 half steps from E ♭ to A ♭ .

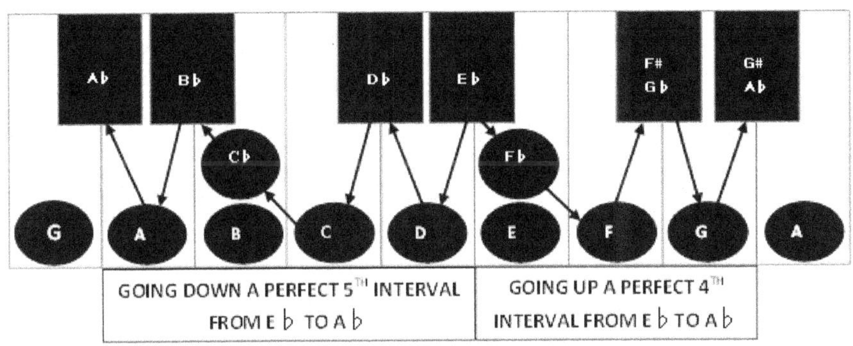

A♭
B♭
C♭
D♭
E♭
F♭
F#
G♭
G#
A♭
G
A
B
C
D
E
F
G
A
GOING DOWN A PERFECT 5TH INTERVAL FROM E♭ TO A♭
GOING UP A PERFECT 4TH INTERVAL FROM E♭ TO A♭

CHAPTER 5

FIGURING OUT TYPES OF CHORDS IN THE D MINOR KEY USING MIRROR

*Let us take D to be:

●A minor key.

●Note number 1 or tonic of our D minor key/scale.

●The i chord in our D minor key/scale.

●The root note of our i chord.

●We need to create the D minor scale both on paper and on keyboard. The underlined letters form the minor scale and we will follow the pattern used to create any minor scale of whole step, half step, whole step, whole step, half step, whole step, whole step.

●Remember we are on the flat side of the mirror.

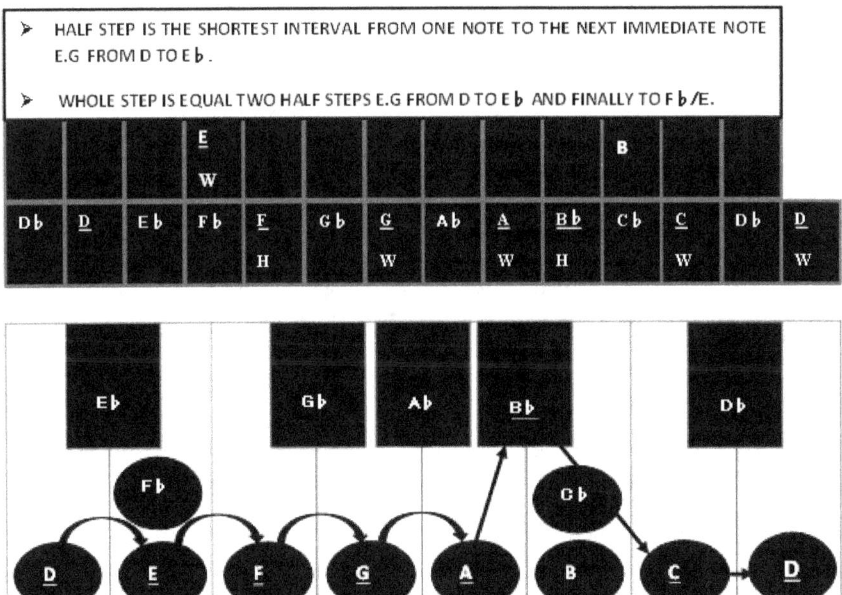

THE D MINOR SCALE

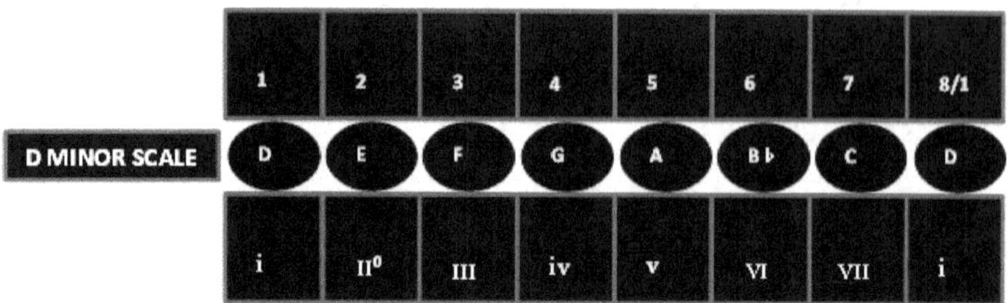

●To know which chords are minor, major or diminished let's look into our mirror.

●Looking at line 3 letters to the left and right of D are minor chords including D itself.

●Now let us start at D which is note number one in our D minor key/scale.

●This is going to be our D minor chord and we are going to designate it the lowercase Roman numeral i.

●To the right of D we have the note A which is note number 5 in our D minor scale.

●This is going to be our A minor chord and we are going to designate it the lowercase Roman numeral v.

●Now going up one letter to the right of D as we have done, is going up a perfect 5th interval which is equal to 7 half steps on the keyboard from D to A which is the same as going down a perfect 4th interval which is equal to going down 5 half steps on the keyboard from D to A.

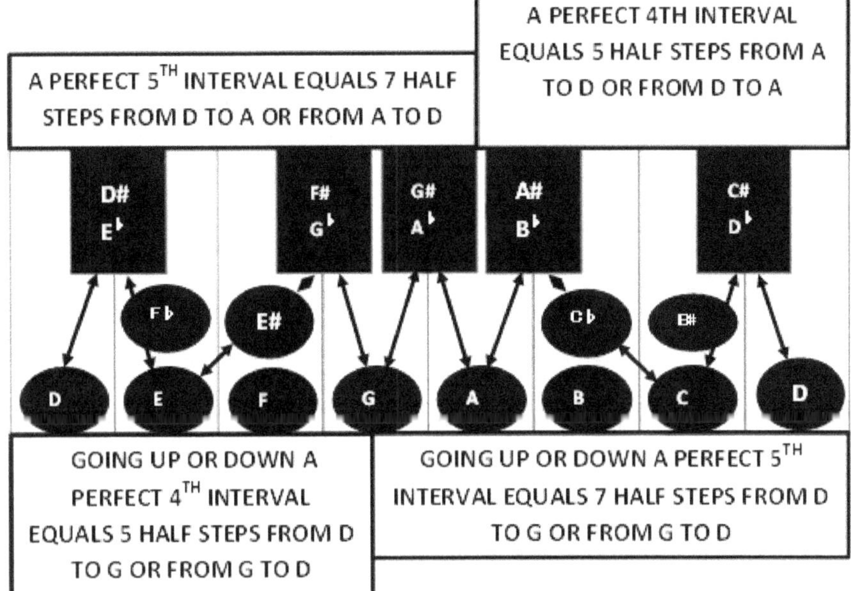

●To the left of D is G which is note number 4 on our D minor scale.

●This is going to be our G minor chord and we are going to designate it the lowercase Roman numeral iv.

●Now going down one letter to the left of D as we have done here is going down a perfect 5th interval which is equal to 7 half steps from D to G on the keyboard. This is the same as going up a perfect 4th interval which is equal to 5 half steps from D to G on the keyboard.

●To know our major chords from the mirror we will count one letter to the left of G we will land on C, one letter to the left of C, we land on F and finally one letter to the left of F we land on B ♭ .

●And we have C, F and B ♭ as our 3 major chords.

●Now what we are doing here is that we are going down in perfect 5ths intervals from G to C to F to B ♭ .

•Now C is note number 7 in our D minor scale and we will designate it the uppercase Roman numeral VII.

•Note F is note number 3 in our D minor scale and we will designate it the uppercase Roman numeral III.

•Note B♭ is note number 6 in our D minor scale and we will designate it the uppercase Roman numeral VI.

•Finally going one letter up to the right of A along line 3 is going up a perfect 5th interval which is equal to going up 7 half steps from A to E on the keyboard, we have the last chord which is E diminished.

•E is note number 2 in our D minor scale.

•So we will designate it the lowercase Roman number ii^0 with a small circle on top to distinguish it as a diminished chord.

FIGURING OUT THE NOTES OF THE TRIAD CHORDS IN D MINOR KEY USING THE MIRROR INDIRECTLY

•Let us start with our i chord which is D minor chord.

•Looking at our mirror we already have two notes D and A.

•The first note D is called the root note of the chord.

•The last note A is called the 5th because it's a perfect 5th interval away from the root note of our chord.

•Now we need to find the middle note which is called the 3rd because it's a 3rd interval away from the root note D.

•It can either be a major or minor 3rd interval away from the root note.

•Since this is a minor chord the middle note is a minor 3rd interval away from the root note of our chord.

•The root note of our chord is D.

•We shall apply this principle of 3rds intervals for all the other chords in our D minor key/scale so as to find out their middle notes.

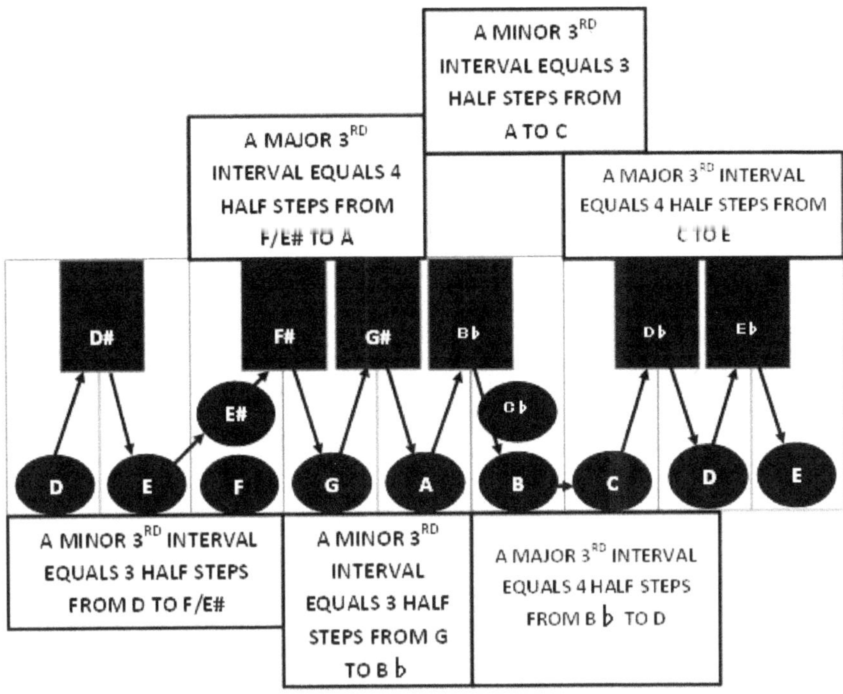

CHORD NUMBER	CHORD NAME	MIDDLE NOTE OR THE 3RD IS A MAJOR OR MINOR 3RD AWAY FROM THE ROOT NOTE.	NOTES
i	D minor	DF	DFA
ii°	E diminished	E??	EGBb
III	F major	FA	FAC
iv	G minor	GBb	GBbD
v	A minor	AC	ACE
VI	Bb major	BbD	BbDF
VII	C major	CE	CEG

•Now you may wonder why we don't spell the D minor chord as DE#A.

•This is because we don't have an E# in our D minor scale/key.

31

•Now what this tells us is that chords are spelled using notes in a specific major or minor key/scale only.

•Now for the E diminished chord the second note has to be a major 3rd interval away from the root note E of our chord. This note is G#.

•The last note is always a perfect 5th interval away from the root note E of our chord. This note is B.

•We then lower these two notes the 3rd and the 5th by a half step.

•This spells the E diminished chord as EGB ♭ .

•The diminished chord is thus formed: Root + minor 3rd + diminished 5th OR

•The diminished chord is thus formed: Root + Flattened 3rd + Flattened 5th.

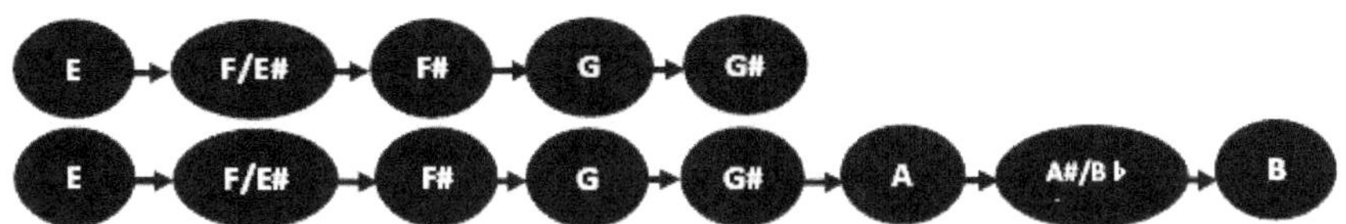

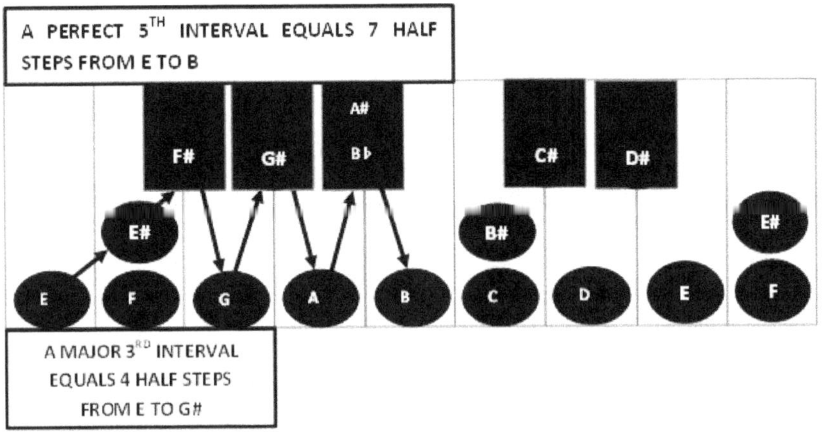

FIGURING OUT THE NOTES OF THE TRIAD CHORDS IN D MINOR KEY USING THE MIRROR DIRECTLY

•Just by looking at our mirror we already have the first note which is the root and the last note which is the 5th. All we have to do is to find our middle note.

1. D MINOR CHORD D?A

•To find the middle note or a minor 3rd interval away from D.

•We will start counting at D along line 2 and go up 5 letters to the right landing on F#.

•This is going up in perfect 5ths intervals which is equal to 7 half steps from letter to letter on the mirror.

•Now since this is minor chord we will lower the F# by a half step to F.

•This effectively spells out the D minor chord as DFA.

2. E DIMINISHED CHORD E??

•How do we find our middle note the 3rd and our last note the 5th?

•Now the middle note or 3rd is a minor 3rd interval away from the root note E.

•The last note which is the 5th is a diminished 5th interval away from the root note E.

• To find our middle note we will start counting at E along line 3 and go up 5 letters to the right landing on G# along line 3.

•Now this is going up in perfect 5ths intervals which is equal to 7 half steps from letter to letter on the mirror.

•Now since this note is a minor 3rd interval away from the root note E we will lower the G# by a half step to G.

•Now for our last note or the 5th we will start counting at E and as usual just by looking at our mirror we already have our first note the root E and our last note the 5th B.

•So starting at E we will go up one letter to the right.

•This is going up a perfect 5th interval which is equal to going up 7 half steps on the keyboard from E to B.

•Now we lower the B by a half step to B ♭ .

•This spells our E diminished chord as EGB ♭ .

3. F MAJOR CHORD F?C

•To find our middle note or a major 3rd interval away from F.

•We will start counting at F along line 3 and go up 5 letters to the right landing on A.

•This is going up in perfect 5ths intervals which is equal to 7 half steps from letter to letter on the mirror.

•This effectively spells out the F major chord as FAC.

4. G MINOR CHORD G?D

•To find our middle note or a minor 3rd interval away from G.

•We will start counting at G along line 2 and go up 5 letters to the right of G landing us on B.

•This is going up in perfect 5ths intervals which is equal to 7 half steps from each letter to the next letter on the mirror.

•Now since this is a minor chord we will lower the B by a half step to B ♭ .

•So our G minor chord spells us GB ♭ D.

5. A MINOR CHORD A?E

●To find our middle note or a minor 3rd interval away from A.

●We will start counting at A either on line 2 or 3 and go up 5 letters to the right landing on C# either on line 2 or 3.

●This is going up in perfect 5ths intervals which is equal to 7 half steps from letter to letter on the mirror.

●Now since this is a minor chord we will lower the C# by a half step to C.

●So our A minor chord spells us ACE.

6. B♭ MAJOR CHORD B♭?F#

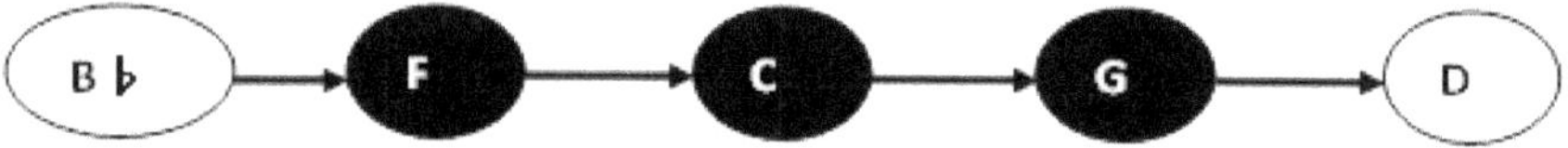

●To find our middle note or a major 3rd interval away from B♭.

●We will start counting at B♭ on line 3 and go up 5 letters to the right landing on D.

●This is going up in perfect 5ths intervals which is equal to 7 half steps from each letter to the next letter on the mirror.

●This effectively spells out our B♭ major chord as B♭DF.

7. C MAJOR CHORD C?G

●To find our middle note or a major 3rd interval away from C.

●We will start counting at C on line 2 and go up 5 letters to the right landing on E.

• This is going up in perfect 5ths intervals which is equal to 7 half steps from each letter to the next letter on the mirror.

• This effectively spells out our C major chord as CEG.

FIGURING OUT TYPES OF CHORDS IN THE F MAJOR KEY USING MIRROR

*Let us take F to be:

• A major key.

• Note number 1 or tonic of our F major key/scale.

• The I chord in our F major key/scale.

• The root note of our I chord.

• We need to create the F major scale both on paper and on keyboard. The underlined letters form the major scale and we will follow the pattern used to create any major scale of whole step, whole step, half step, whole step, whole step, whole step, half step.

• Remember we are on the flat side of our mirror.

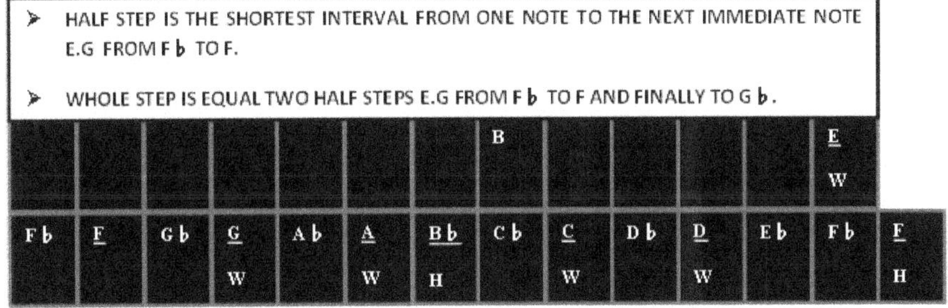

> HALF STEP IS THE SHORTEST INTERVAL FROM ONE NOTE TO THE NEXT IMMEDIATE NOTE E.G FROM F♭ TO F.

> WHOLE STEP IS EQUAL TWO HALF STEPS E.G FROM F♭ TO F AND FINALLY TO G♭.

							B					E
												W
F♭	F	G♭	G	A♭	A	B♭	C♭	C	D♭	D	E♭	F♭	F
			W		W	H		W		W			H

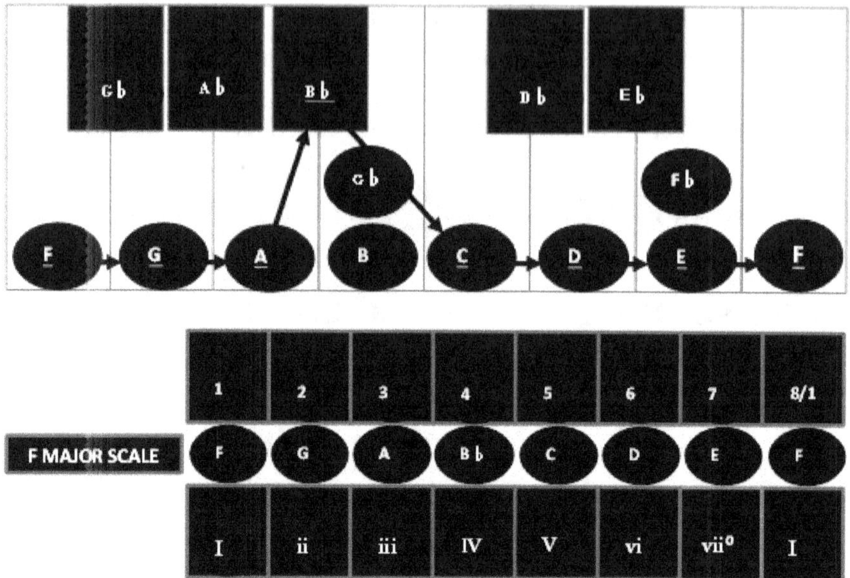

•To know which chords are major, minor or diminished let's look into our mirror.

•Looking at line 3 letters to the left and right of F are major chords including F itself.

•Now let us start at F which is note number one in our F major scale.

•This is going to be our F major chord and we are going to designate it the uppercase Roman numeral I.

•To the right of F we have the note C which is note number 5 in our F major scale.

•This is going to be our C major chord and we are going to designate it the uppercase Roman numeral V.

•Now going up one letter to the right of F as we have done is going up a perfect 5th interval which is equal to 7 half steps from F to C on the keyboard. This is the same as going down a perfect 4th interval which is equal to 5 half steps from F to C on the keyboard.

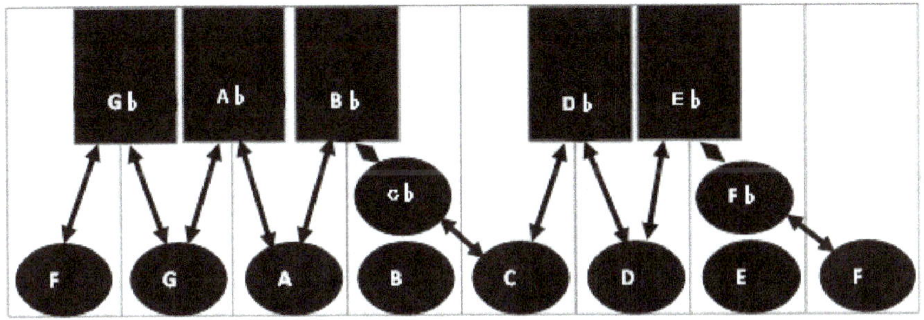

●To the left of F is B♭ which is note number 4 on our F major key/scale. This is going to be our B♭ major chord and we are going to designate it the uppercase Roman numeral IV.

●Now going down one letter to the left of F as we have done here is going down a perfect 5th interval which is equal to 7 half steps from F to B♭ on the key board, this is the same as going up a perfect 4th interval which is equal to 5 half steps from F to B♭ on the keyboard.

●To know our minor chords from the mirror we will count one letter to the right of C we will land on G, one letter to the right of G we land on D and finally one letter to the right of D is A.

●And we have G, D and A as our 3 minor chords.

●Now what we are doing here is that we are going up in perfect 5ths intervals from C to G to D to A.

●Now G is note number 2 in our F major scale and we will designate it the lowercase Roman numeral ii.

●Note D is note number 6 in our F major scale and we will designate it the lowercase Roman numeral vi.

●Note A is note number 3 in our F major scale and we will designate it the lowercase Roman numeral iii.

•Finally going up one letter to the right of A along line 3 is going up a perfect 5th interval which is equal to going up 7 half steps from A to E on the keyboard we have the last chord which is E diminished chord.

•E is note number 7 in our F major scale.

•So, we will designate it the lowercase Roman number vii° with a small circle on top to distinguish it as a diminished chord.

FIGURING OUT THE NOTES OF THE TRIAD CHORDS IN F MAJOR KEY USING THE MIRROR INDIRECTLY

•Let us start with our I chord which is F major chord.

•Looking at our mirror we already have two notes F and C.

•The first note F is called the root of the chord.

•The last note C is called the 5th because it a perfect 5th interval away from the root note.

•Now we need to find the middle note which is called the 3rd because it's a 3rd interval away from the root note.

•It can either be a major or minor 3rd interval away from the root note.

•Our root note here is F.

•We shall apply this principle of 3rds intervals for all the other chords in our F major key/scale so as to find out all their middle notes.

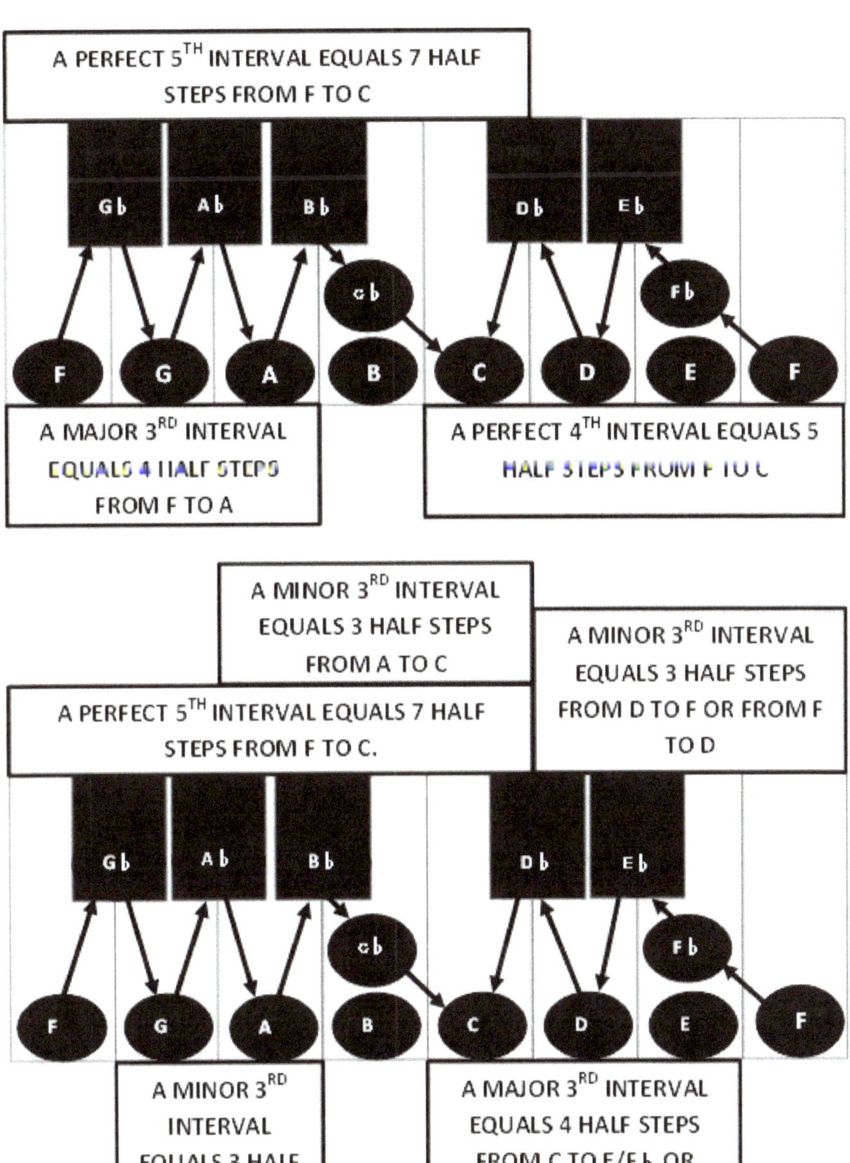

A PERFECT 5TH INTERVAL EQUALS 7 HALF STEPS FROM F TO C
Gb
Ab
Bb
Db
Eb
Gb
Fb
F
G
A
B
C
D
E
F
A MAJOR 3RD INTERVAL EQUALS 4 HALF STEPS FROM F TO A
A PERFECT 4TH INTERVAL EQUALS 5 HALF STEPS FROM F TO C
A MINOR 3RD INTERVAL EQUALS 3 HALF STEPS FROM A TO C
A MINOR 3RD INTERVAL EQUALS 3 HALF STEPS FROM D TO F OR FROM F TO D
A PERFECT 5TH INTERVAL EQUALS 7 HALF STEPS FROM F TO C.
Gb
Ab
Bb
Db
Eb
Gb
Fb
F
G
A
B
C
D
E
F
A MINOR 3RD INTERVAL EQUALS 3 HALF STEPS FROM G TO Bb
A MAJOR 3RD INTERVAL EQUALS 4 HALF STEPS FROM C TO E/Fb OR FROM E/Fb TO C

CHORD NUMBER	CHORD NAME	MIDDLE NOTE OR THE 3RD IS A MAJOR OR MINOR 3RD AWAY FROM THE ROOT NOTE.	NOTES
I	F major	FA	FAC
ii	G minor	GB♭	GB♭D
iii	A minor	AC	ACE
IV	B♭ major	B♭D	B♭DF
V	C major	CE	CEG
vi	D minor	DF	DFA
vii⁰	E diminished	E??	EGB♭

●Now for the E diminished chord the second note has to be a major 3rd interval away from the root note E of our chord. This note is G#.

●The last note is always a perfect 5th interval away from the root note E of our chord. This note is B.

●We then lower these two notes the 3rd and the 5th by a half step.

●This spells the E diminished chord as EGB♭.

●The diminished chord is thus formed: Root + minor 3rd + diminished 5th.

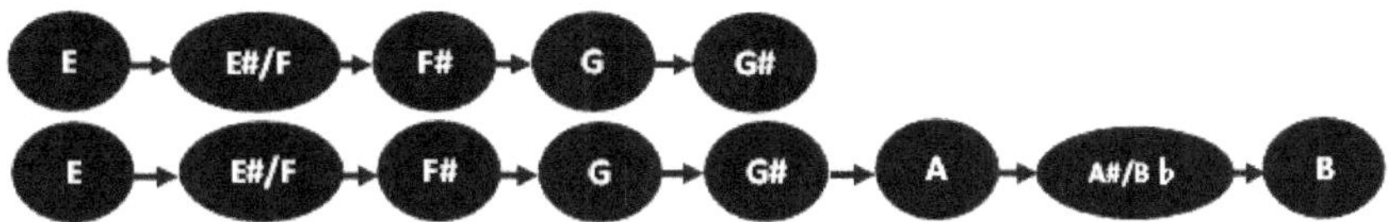

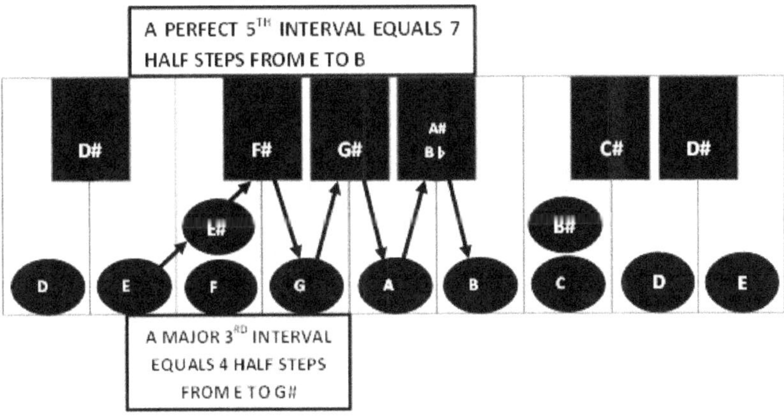

FIGURING OUT THE NOTES OF THE TRIAD CHORDS IN F MAJOR KEY USING THE MIRROR DIRECTLY

• Just by looking at our mirror we already have the first note which is the root and the last note which is the 5th. All we have to do is to find our middle note, the 3rd.

1. F MAJOR CHORD F?C

• To find the middle note or a major 3rd interval away from F.

• We will start counting at F and go up 5 letters to the right landing on A

• This is going up in perfect 5ths intervals which is equal to 7 half steps from letter to letter on the mirror.

• This effectively spells out the F major chord as FAC.

2. G MINOR CHORD G?D

•To find our middle note or a minor 3rd interval away from G.

•We will start counting at G on line 2 and go up 5 letters to the right landing on B.

•This is going up in perfect 5th intervals which is equal to 7 half steps from letter to letter on the mirror.

•Now since this is a minor chord we will lower the B by a half step to B ♭ .

•This effectively spells out the G minor chord as GB ♭ D.

3. A MINOR CHORD A?E

•To find our middle note or a minor 3rd interval away from A.

•We will start counting at A either on line 2 or 3 and go up 5 letters to the right landing on C# either on line 2 or 3.

•This is going up in perfect 5ths intervals which is equal to 7 half steps from letter to letter on the mirror.

•Now since this is a minor chord we will lower the C# by a half step to C.

•This effectively spells out the A minor chord as ACE.

4. B ♭ MAJOR CHORD B ♭ ? F

●To find the middle note or a major 3rd interval away from B ♭ .

●We will start counting at B ♭ on line 3 and go up 5 letters to the right landing on D.

●This is going up in perfect 5ths intervals which is equal to 7 half steps from letter to letter on the mirror.

●This effectively spells out the B ♭ major chord as B ♭ DF.

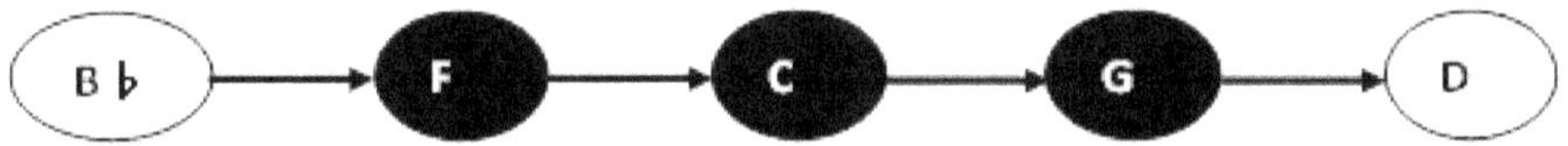

5. C MAJOR CHORD C?G

●To find our middle note or a major 3rd interval away from C.

●We will start counting at C on line 2 and go up 5 letters to the right landing on E.

●This is going up in perfect 5ths intervals which is equal to 7 half steps from letter to letter on the mirror.

●So, our C major chord spells us CEG.

6. D MINOR CHORD D?A

●To find our middle note or a minor 3rd interval away from D.

●We will start counting at D along line 2 and go up 5 letters to the right landing on F#.

●This is going up in perfect 5ths intervals which is equal to 7 half steps from letter to letter on the mirror.

•Now since this is a minor chord we will lower the F# by a half step to F.

•This effectively spells out our D minor chord as DFA.

7. E DIMINISHED CHORD E??

•How do we find our middle note the 3rd and our last note the 5th?

•Now the middle note or 3rd is a minor 3rd interval away from the root note E.

•The last note which is the 5th is a diminished 5th interval away from the root note E.

•We will start counting at E along line 2 or 3 and go up 5 letters to the right landing on G#.

•Now this is going up in perfect 5ths intervals which is equal to 7 half steps from letter to letter on the mirror.

•Now since this note is a minor 3rd interval away from the root note E we will lower the G# by a half step to G.

•Now for our last note or the 5th we will start counting at E and as usual just by looking at our mirror we already have our first note the root E and our last note the 5th B.

•So, starting at E we will go up one letter to the right.

•This is going up a perfect 5th interval which is equal to 7 half steps from E to B on the mirror.

•Now we lower the B by a half step to B ♭ .

●This spells our E diminished chord as EGB♭.

FIGURING OUT TYPES OF CHORDS IN THE C MAJOR KEY USING MIRROR

*Let us take C to be:

●A major key.

●Note number 1 or tonic of our C major key/scale.

●The I chord in our C major key/scale.

●The root note of our I chord.

●We need to create the C major scale both on paper and on keyboard. The underlined letters form the major scale and we will follow the pattern used to create any major scale of whole step, whole step, half step, whole step, whole step, whole step, half step.

●We can start on either side of the mirror, the sharp side or the flat side.

●This is because C is a neutral key and it has no sharps or flats in its key signature.

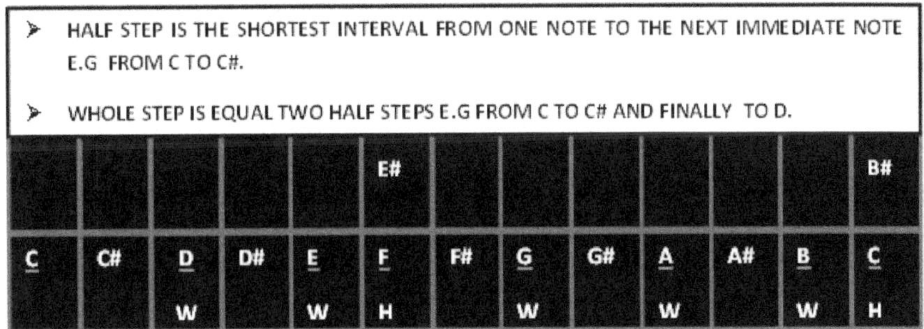

> HALF STEP IS THE SHORTEST INTERVAL FROM ONE NOTE TO THE NEXT IMMEDIATE NOTE E.G FROM C TO C#.

> WHOLE STEP IS EQUAL TWO HALF STEPS E.G FROM C TO C# AND FINALLY TO D.

C	C#	D	D#	E	F	F#	G	G#	A	A#	B	C
					(E#)						(B#)	
		W		W	H		W		W		W	H

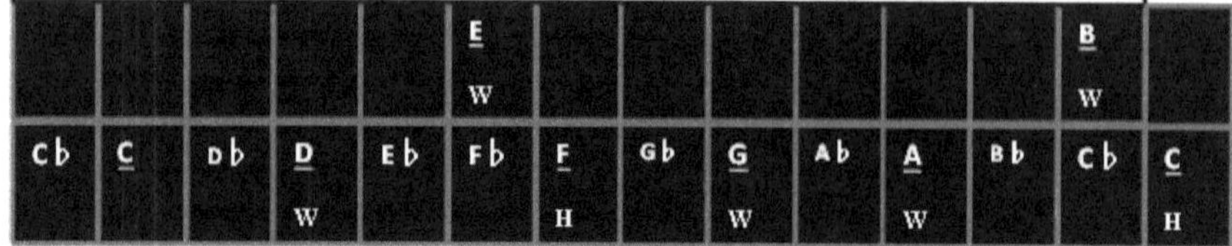

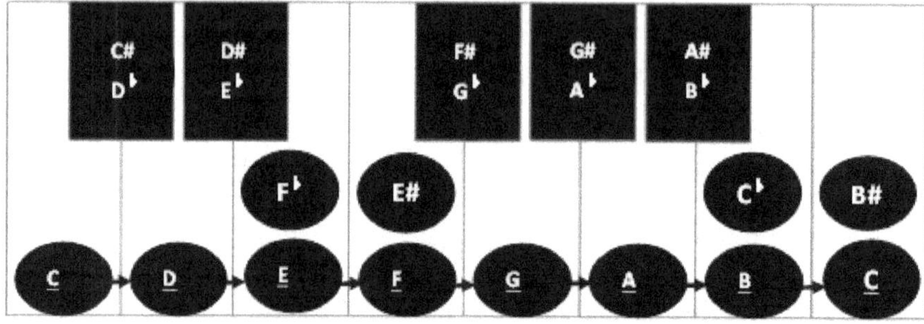

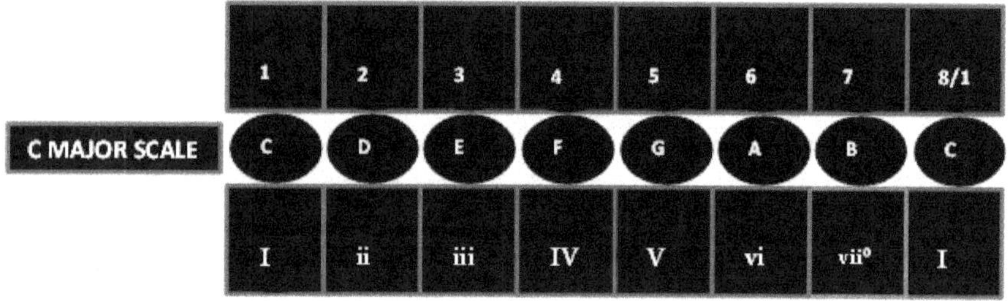

•To know which chords are major, minor or diminished let's look into our mirror.

•Looking at line 2 letters to the left and right of C either on the sharp side or the flat side of the mirror are major chords including C itself.

•Now let us start at C which is note number one in our C major key/ scale.

•This is going to be our C major chord and we are going to designate it the uppercase Roman numeral I.

•To the right of C we have the note G which is note number 5 in our C major scale.

•This is going to be our G major chord and we are going to designate it the uppercase Roman numeral V.

•Now going up one letter to the right of C as we have done is going up a perfect 5th interval which is equal to 7 half steps on the keyboard from C to G, this is the same as going down a perfect 4th interval which is equal to 5 half steps from C to G.

•To the left of C is F which is note number 4 on our C major key/scale. This is going to be our F major chord and we are going to designate it the uppercase Roman numeral IV.

•Now going down one letter to the left of C as we have done here is going down a perfect 5th interval which is equal to 7 half steps from C to F on the keyboard. This is the same as going up a perfect 4th interval which is equal to 5 half steps from C to F.

•To know our minor chords from the mirror we will count one letter to the right of G we will land on D, one letter to the right of D we land on A and finally one letter to the right of A we land on E.

•And we have D, A, and E as our 3 minor chords.

•Now what we are doing here is that we are going up in perfect 5ths intervals from G to D to A to E.

•Now D is note number 2 in our C major scale and we will designate it the lowercase Roman numeral ii.

•Note A is note number 6 in our C major scale and we will designate it the lowercase Roman numeral vi.

•Note E is note number 3 in our C major scale and we will designate it the lowercase Roman numeral iii.

•Finally going up one letter to the right of E which is going up a perfect 5th interval we have the last chord which is B diminished.

•B is note number 7 in our C major scale.

•So, we will designate it the lowercase Roman numeral vii^0 with a small circle on top to distinguish it as a diminished chord.

FIGURING OUT THE NOTES OF THE TRIAD CHORDS IN C MAJOR KEY USING THE MIRROR INDIRECTLY

•Let us start with our I chord which is C major chord.

•Looking at our mirror we already have two notes C and G.

•The first note C is called the root of the chord.

•The last note G is called the 5th because it's a perfect 5th interval away from the root.

•Now we need to find the middle note which is called the 3rd because it's a 3rd interval away from the root note.

•It can either be a major or minor 3rd interval away from the root note.

•Our root note here is C.

•We shall apply this principle of 3rds intervals for all the other chords in our C major key/scale so as to find out their middle notes.

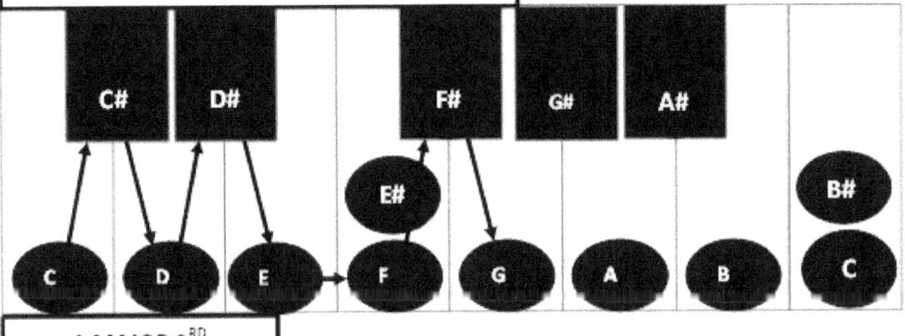

A PERFECT 5TH INTERVAL EQUALS 7 HALF STEPS FROM C TO G.
C#
D#
F#
G#
A#
E#
B#
C
D
E
F
G
A
B
C
A MAJOR 3RD INTERVAL EQUALS 4 HALF STEPS FROM C TO E

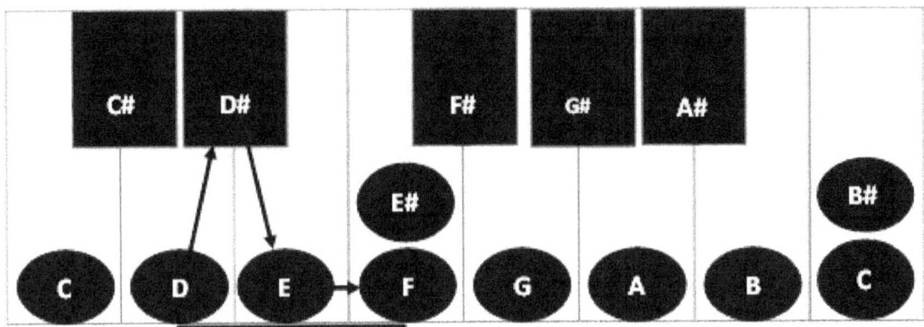

C#
D#
F#
G#
A#
E#
B#
C
D
E
F
G
A
B
C
A MINOR 3RD INTERVAL EQUALS 3 HALF STEPS FROM D TO F/E#

CHORD NUMBER	CHORD NAME	MIDDLE NOTE OR THE 3RD IS A MAJOR OR MINOR 3RD AWAY FROM THE ROOT NOTE.	NOTES
I	C major	CE	CEG
ii	D minor	DF	DFA
iii	E minor	EG	EGB
IV	F major	FA	FAC
V	G major	GB	GBD
vi	A minor	AC	ACE
vii°	B diminished	B??	BDF

●Now for the B diminished chord the second note has to be a major 3rd interval away from the root note B of our chord. This note is D#.

●The last note is always a perfect 5th interval away from the root note B of our chord. This note is F#.

●We then lower these two notes the 3rd and the 5th by a half step.

●This spells the B diminished chord as BDF.

●The diminished chord is thus formed: Root + minor 3rd + diminished 5th.

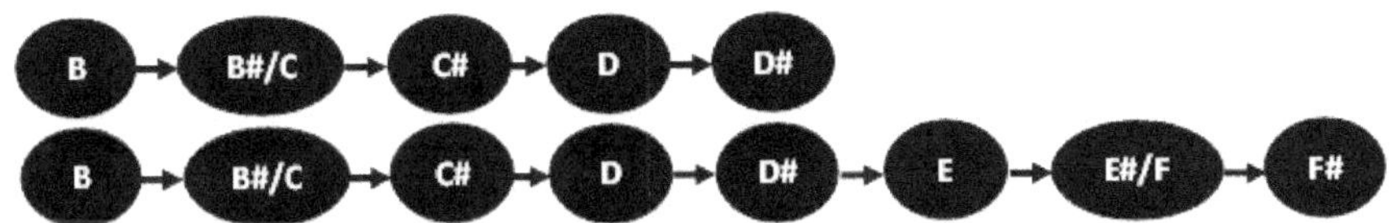

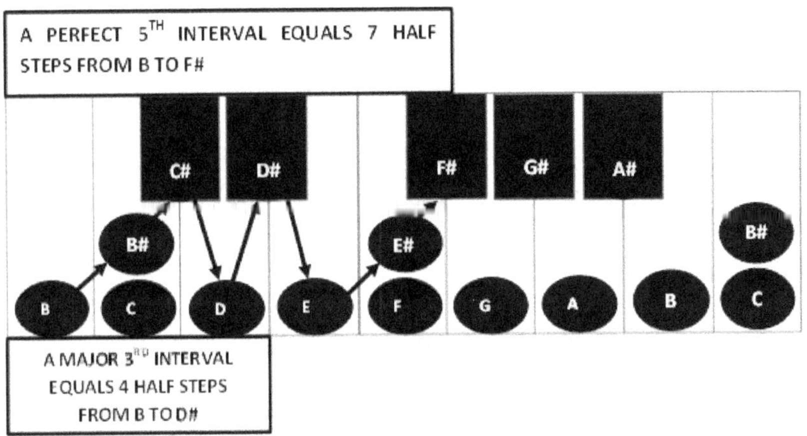

FIGURING OUT THE NOTES OF THE TRIAD CHORDS IN C MAJOR KEY USING THE MIRROR DIRECTLY

1. C MAJOR CHORD C?G

- To find the middle note or a major 3rd interval away from C.

- We will start counting at C along line 2 and go up 5 letters to the right landing on E.

- This is going up in perfect 5ths intervals from letter to letter on the mirror.

- This effectively spells out the C major chord as CEG.

2. D MINOR CHORD D?A

- To find our middle note or a minor 3rd interval away from D.

•We will start counting at D and go up 5 letters to the right landing on F# on line 2.

•This is going up in perfect 5ths intervals.

•Now since this is a minor chord we will lower the F# by a half step to F.

•This effectively spells out the D minor chord as DFA.

3. E MINOR CHORD E?B

•To find our middle note or a minor 3rd interval away from E.

•We will start counting at E along line 3 and go up 5 letters to the right landing on G#.

•This is going up in perfect 5ths intervals from letter to letter on the mirror.

•Now since this is a minor chord we will lower the G# by a half step to G.

•This effectively spells out the E minor chord as EGB.

4. F MAJOR CHORD F?C

•To find our middle note or a major 3rd interval away from F.

•We will start counting at F along line 3 and go up 5 letters to the right of F landing us on A.

•This is going up in perfect 5ths intervals from letter to letter on the mirror.

•So our F major chord spells us FAC.

5. G MAJOR CHORD G?D

•To find our middle note or a major 3rd interval away from G.

•We will start counting at G and go up 5 letters to the right landing on B.

•This is going up in perfect 5ths intervals from letter to letter on the mirror.

•So our G major chord spells us GBD.

6. A MINOR CHORD A?E

•To find our middle note or a minor 3rd interval away from A.

•We will start counting at A along line 2 or 3 and go up 5 letters to the right landing on C# either on line 2 or 3.

•This is going up in perfect 5ths intervals which is equal to 7 half steps from letter to letter on the mirror.

•Now since this is a minor chord we will lower the C# by a half step to C.

•This effectively spells out our A minor chord as ACE.

7. B DIMINISHED CHORD B??

•How do we find our middle note the 3rd and our last note the 5th?

•Now the middle note or 3rd is a minor 3rd interval away from the root note B.

•The last note which is the 5th is a diminished 5th interval away from the root note B.

•We will start counting at B along line 3 and go up 5 letters to the right landing on D#.

•Now this is going up in perfect 5ths intervals which is equal to 7 half steps from letter to letter on the mirror.

•Now since this note is a minor 3rd interval away from the root note B we will lower the D# by a half step to D.

•Now for our last note or the 5th we will start counting at B and as usual just by looking at our mirror we already have our first note the root B and our last note the 5th F#.

•So, starting at B we will go up one letter to the right.

•This is going up a perfect 5th interval which is equal to 7 half steps from B to F# on the keyboard.

•Now we lower the F# by a half step to F.

•This spells our B diminished chord as BDF.

FIGURING OUT TYPES OF CHORDS IN THE a♭ MINOR KEY USING MIRROR

*Let us take A♭ to be:

●A minor key.

●Note number 1 or tonic of our A♭ minor key/scale.

●The i chord in our A♭ minor key/scale.

●The root note of our i chord.

●We need to create the A♭ minor scale both on paper and on keyboard. The underlined letters form the minor scale and we will follow the pattern used to create any minor scale of whole step, half step, whole step, whole step, half step, whole step, whole step.

●Remember now that we are in the flat side of the mirror.

> HALF STEP IS THE SHORTEST INTERVAL FROM ONE NOTE TO THE NEXT IMMEDIATE NOTE E.G FROM B♭ TO B/C♭.
>
> WHOLE STEP IS EQUAL TWO HALF STEPS E.G FROM A♭ TO A AND FINALLY TO B♭.

A♭	A	B♭	C♭	C	D♭	D	E♭	F♭	F	G♭	G	A♭
		W	H		W		W	H		W		W

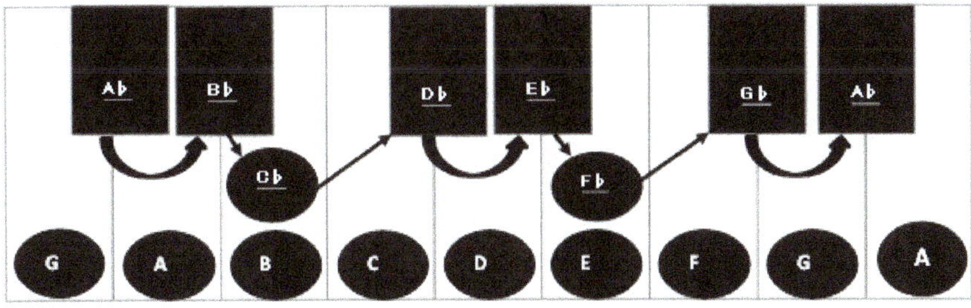

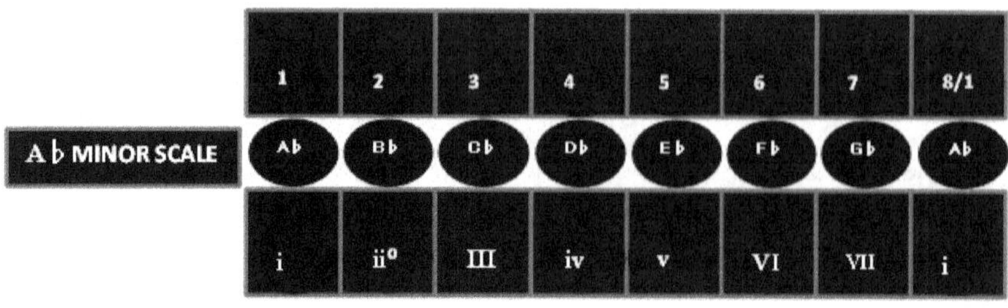

●To know which chords are minor, major or diminished let's look into our mirror.

●Looking at line 1, 2 or 3 letters to the left and right of A♭ are minor chords including A♭ itself.

●Now let us start at A♭ which is note number one in our A♭ minor scale.

●This is going to be our A♭ minor chord and we are going to designate it the lowercase Roman numeral i.

●To the right of A♭ we have the note E♭ which is note number 5 in our A♭ minor scale.

●This is going to be our E♭ minor chord and we are going to designate it the lowercase Roman numeral v.

●Now going up one letter to the right of A♭ as we have done is going up a perfect 5th interval which is equal to 7 half steps on the keyboard from A♭ to E♭. This is the same as going down a perfect 4th interval on the keyboard which is equal to 5 half steps from A♭ to E♭.

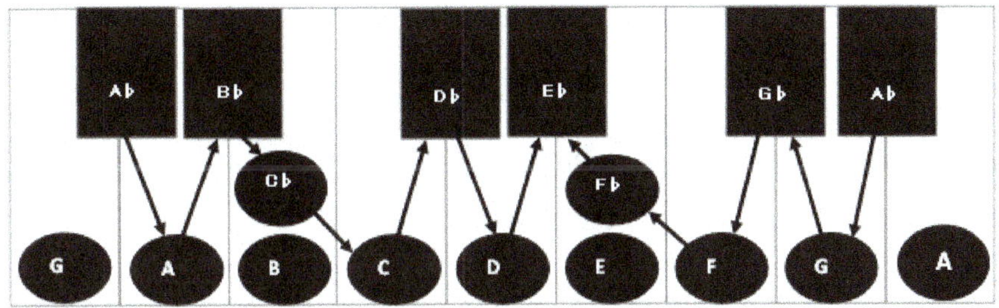

•To the left of A♭ is D♭ which is note number 4 on our A♭ minor key/scale. This is going to be our D♭ minor chord and we are going to designate it the lowercase Roman numeral iv.

•Now going down one letter to the left of A♭ as we have done here is going down a perfect 5th interval which is equal to 7 half steps from A♭ to D♭ on the keyboard.

•This is the same as going up a perfect 4th interval which is equal to 5 half steps from A♭ to D♭ on the keyboard.

•So our 3 minor chords are A♭ , E♭ and D♭ .

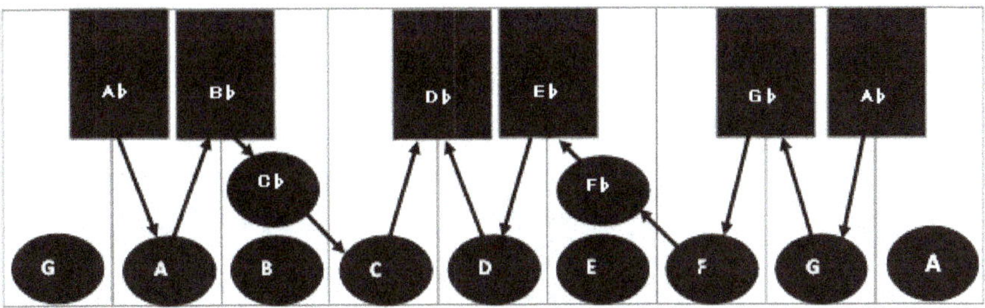

•To know our major chords from the mirror we will count one letter to the left of D♭ along line 1 we will land on G♭ one letter to the left of G♭ we land on C♭ and finally one letter to the left of C♭ we land on F♭ .

•And we have G♭ , C♭ , and F♭ as our 3 major chords.

•Now what we are doing here is that we are going down in perfect 5ths intervals from D ♭ to G ♭ to C ♭ to F ♭ .

•Now G ♭ is note number 7 in our A ♭ minor scale and we will designate it the uppercase Roman numeral VII.

•Note C ♭ is note number 3 in our A ♭ minor scale and we will designate it the uppercase Roman numeral III.

•Note F ♭ is note number 6 in our A ♭ minor scale and we will designate it the uppercase Roman numeral VI.

•Finally going up one letter up to the right of E ♭ is going up a perfect 5th interval which is equal to going up 7 half steps on the keyboard from E ♭ to B ♭ , we have the last chord which is B ♭ diminished.

•Or you can go down a perfect 4th interval which is equal to 5 half steps from E ♭ to B ♭ on the keyboard.

•B ♭ is note number 2 in our A ♭ minor scale. So we will designate it the lowercase Roman number ii⁰ with a small circle on top to distinguish it as a diminished chord.

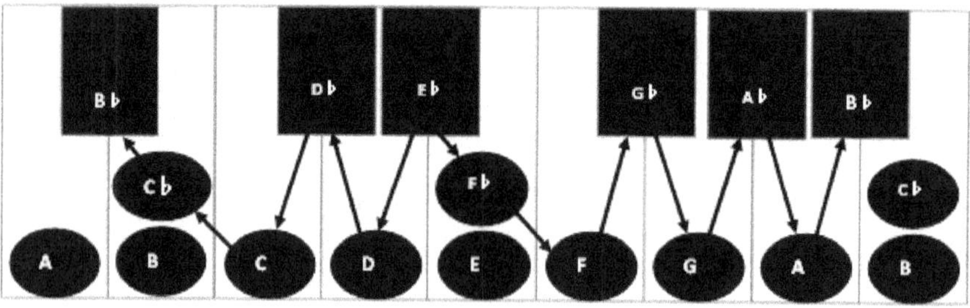

FIGURING OUT THE NOTES OF THE TRIAD CHORDS IN A ♭ MINOR KEY USING THE MIRROR INDIRECTLY

●Let us start with our i chord which is A ♭ minor chord.

●Looking at our mirror we already have two notes A ♭ and E ♭ .

●The first note A ♭ is called the root of the chord.

●The last note E ♭ is called the 5th because it's a perfect 5th interval away from the root.

●Now we need to find the middle note which is called the 3rd because it's a 3rd interval away from the root note.

●It can either be a major or minor 3rd interval away from the root note.

●Our root note here is A ♭ .

●We shall apply this principle of 3rds intervals for all the other chords in our A ♭ minor key/scale so as to find out their middle notes.

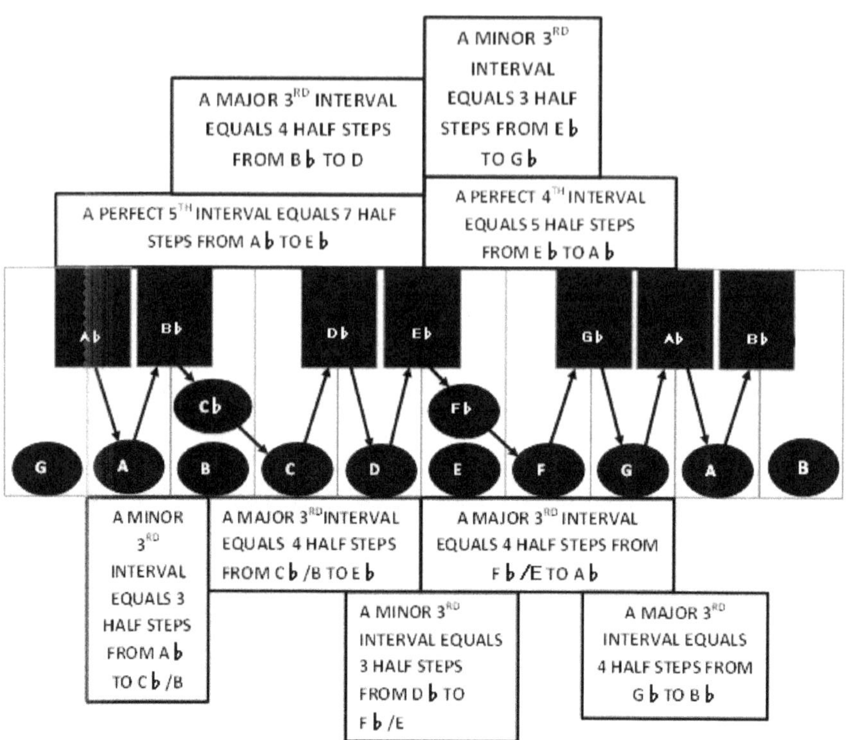

CHORD NUMBER	CHORD NAME	MIDDLE NOTE OR THE 3RD IS A MAJOR OR MINOR 3RD AWAY FROM THE ROOT NOTE.	NOTES
i	A♭ minor	A♭ C♭	A♭ C♭ E♭
ii°	B♭ diminished	B♭ ??	B♭ D♭ F♭
III	C♭ major	C♭ E♭	C♭ E♭ G♭
iv	D♭ minor	D♭ F♭	D♭ F♭ A♭
v	E♭ minor	E♭ G♭	E♭ G♭ B♭
VI	F♭ major	F♭ A♭	F♭ A♭ C♭
VII	G♭ major	G♭ B♭	G♭ B♭ D♭

●Now for the B♭ diminished chord the second note has to be a major 3rd interval away from the root note B♭ of our chord. This note is D.

●The last note is always a perfect 5th interval away from the root note B♭ of our chord. This note is F.

●We then lower these two notes the 3rd and the 5th by a half step.

•This spells the B♭ diminished chord as B♭ D♭ F♭.

•The diminished chord is thus formed: Root + minor 3rd + diminished 5th.

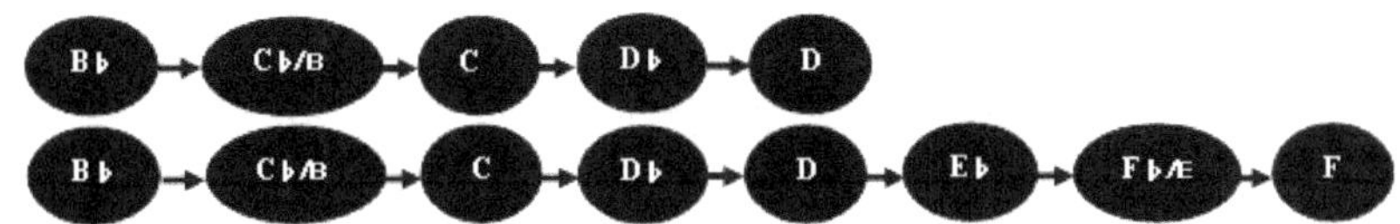

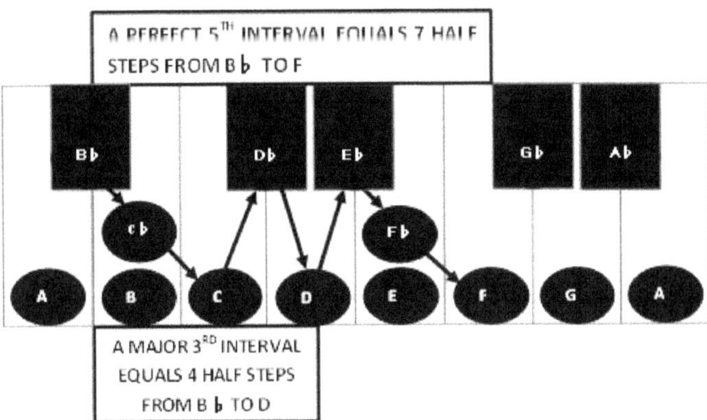

FIGURING OUT THE NOTES OF THE TRIAD CHORDS IN A♭ MINOR KEY USING THE MIRROR DIRECTLY

•Just by looking at our mirror we already have the first note which is the root and the last note which is the 5th. All we have to do is to find our middle note.

1. A♭ MINOR CHORD A♭ ? E♭

•To find the middle note or a minor 3rd interval away from A♭.

•We will start counting at A♭ along line 3 and go up 5 letters to the right landing on C.

•This is going up in perfect 5ths intervals which is equal to 7 half steps from letter to letter on the mirror.

●Now since this is a minor chord we will lower the C by a half step to C ♭ .

●This effectively spells out the A ♭ minor chord as A ♭ C ♭ E ♭ .

2. B ♭ DIMINISHED CHORD B ♭ ??

●How do we find our middle note the 3rd and our last note the 5th?

●Now the middle note or 3rd is a minor 3rd interval away from the root note B ♭ .

●The last note which is the 5th is a diminished 5th interval away from the root note B ♭ .

●We will start counting at B ♭ along line 3 and go up 5 letters to the right landing on D along line 3.

●Now this is going up in perfect 5ths intervals which is equal to 7 half steps from letter to letter on the mirror.

●Now since this note is a minor 3rd interval away from the root note B ♭ we will lower the D by a half step to D ♭ .

●Now for our last note or the 5th we will start counting at B ♭ and as usual just by looking at our mirror we already have our first note the root B ♭ and our last note the 5th F.

●So starting at B ♭ we will go up one letter to the right.

●This is going up a perfect 5th interval which is equal to 7 half steps on the key board landing us on F.

●Now we lower the F by a half step to F ♭ .

●This spells our B ♭ diminished chord as B ♭ D ♭ F ♭ .

3. C ♭ MAJOR CHORD C ♭ ? G ♭

●To find our middle note or a major 3rd interval away from C ♭ .

●We will start counting at C ♭ either on line 1 or 2 and go up 5 letters to the right landing on E ♭ .

●This is going up in perfect 5ths intervals which is equal to 7 half steps from letter to letter on the mirror.

●This effectively spells out the C ♭ major chord as C ♭ E ♭ G ♭ .

4. D ♭ MINOR CHORD D ♭ ? A ♭

●To find our middle note or a minor 3rd interval away from D ♭ .

●We will start counting at D ♭ along line 2 and go up 5 letters to the right of D ♭ landing us on F.

●This is going up in perfect 5ths intervals which is equal to 7 half steps from letter to letter on the mirror.

●Now since this is a minor chord we will lower the F by a half step to F ♭ .

●So our D ♭ minor chord spells us D ♭ F ♭ A ♭ .

5. E♭ MINOR CHORD E♭ ? B♭

●To find our middle note or a minor 3rd interval away from E♭.

●We will start counting at E♭ along line 3 and go up 5 letters to the right landing on G.

●This is going up in perfect 5ths intervals which is equal to 7 half steps from letter to letter on the mirror.

●Now since this is a minor chord we will lower the G by a half step to G♭.

●So our E♭ minor chord spells us E♭ G♭ B♭.

6. F♭ MAJOR CHORD F♭ ? C♭

●To find our middle note or a major 3rd interval away from F♭.

●We will start counting at F♭ along line 1 and go up 5 letters to the right landing on A♭.

●This is going up in perfect 5ths intervals which is equal to 7 half steps from letter to letter on the mirror.

●This effectively spells out our F♭ major chord as F♭ A♭ C♭.

7. G♭ MAJOR CHORD G♭? D♭

•To find our middle note or a major 3rd interval away from G♭.

•We will start counting at G♭ along line 1 or 2 and go up 5 letters to the right landing on B♭.

•This is going up in perfect 5ths intervals which are equal to 7 half steps from letter to letter on the mirror.

•This effectively spells out our G♭ major chord as G♭ B♭ D♭.

FIGURING OUT TYPES OF CHORDS IN THE A MINOR KEY USING MIRROR

*Let us take A to be:

•A minor key.

•Note number 1 or tonic of our A minor key/scale.

•The i chord in our A minor key/scale.

•The root note of our i chord.

•We need to create the A minor scale both on paper and on keyboard. The underlined letters form the minor scale and we will follow the pattern used to create any minor scale of whole step, half step, whole step, whole step, half step, whole step, whole step.

•We can start on either side of the mirror, the sharp side or the flat side.

•This is because A minor is a neutral key and it has no sharps or flats in its key signature.

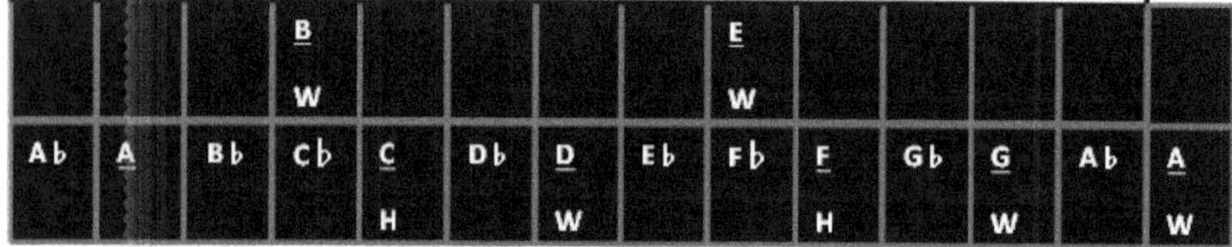

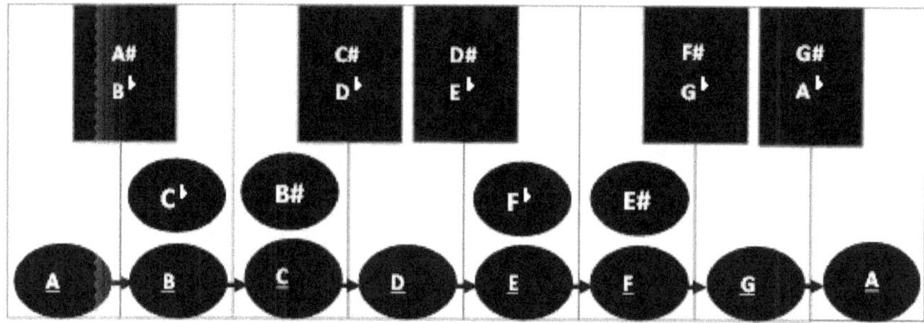

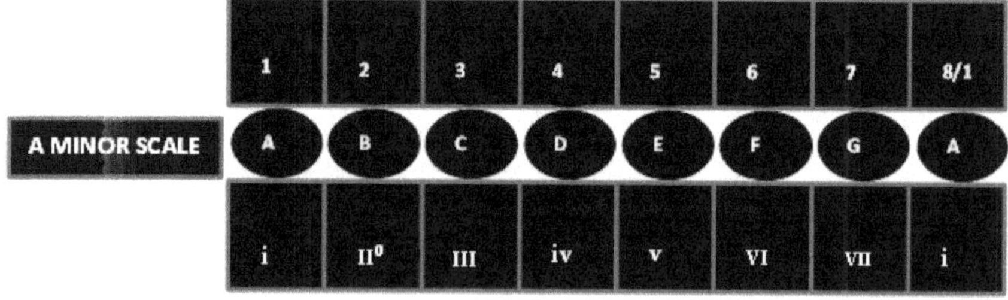

●To know which chords are minor, major or diminished let's look into our mirror.

●Looking at line 3 letters to the left and right of A are minor chords including A itself.

•Now let us start at A which is note number one in our A minor key/ scale.

•This is going to be our A minor chord and we are going to designate it the lowercase Roman numeral i.

•To the right of A we have the note E which is note number 5 in our A minor scale.

•This is going to be our E minor chord and we are going to designate it the lowercase Roman numeral v.

•Now going up one letter to the right of A as we have done is going up a perfect 5th interval which is equal to 7 half steps on the keyboard from A to E. This is the same as going down a perfect 4th interval, which is equal to 5 half steps on the keyboard from A to E.

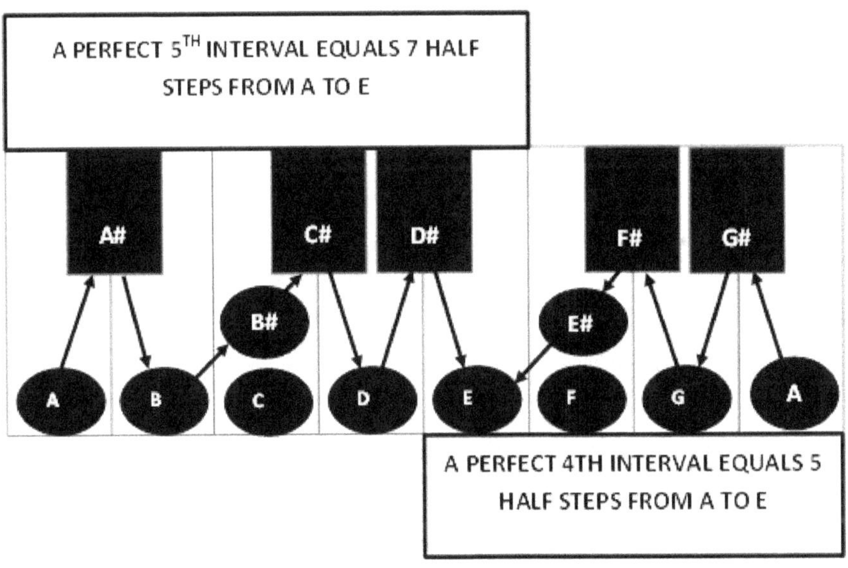

•To the left of A is D which is note number 4 on our A minor key/scale. This is going to be our D minor chord and we are going to designate it the lowercase Roman numeral iv.

•Now going down one letter to the left of A as we have done here is going down a perfect 5th interval which is equal to 7 half steps from A to D on the keyboard. This is the same as going up a perfect 4th interval which is equal to 5 half steps from A to D on the keyboard.

•To know our major chords from the mirror we will count one letter to the left of D we will land on G one letter to the left of G we land on C and finally one letter to the left of C we land on F.

•And we have G, C, and F as our 3 major chords.

•Now what we are doing here is that we are going down in perfect 5ths intervals from D to G to C to F.

•Now G is note number 7 in our A minor scale and we will designate it the uppercase Roman numeral VII.

•Note C is note number 3 in our A minor scale and we will designate it the uppercase Roman numeral III.

•Note F is note number 6 in our A minor scale and we will designate it the uppercase Roman numeral VI.

•Finally going one letter up to the right of E which is going up a perfect 5th interval we have the last chord which is B diminished.

•B is note number 2 in our A minor scale.

•So we will designate it the lowercase Roman numeral ii^0 with a small circle on top to distinguish it as a diminished chord.

FIGURING OUT THE NOTES OF THE TRIAD CHORDS IN A MINOR KEY USING THE MIRROR INDIRECTLY

•Let us start with our i chord which is A minor chord.

•Looking at our mirror we already have two notes A and E.

●The first note A is called the root of the chord.

●The last note E is called the 5th because it's a perfect 5th interval away from the root.

●Now we need to find the middle note which is called the 3rd because it's a 3rd interval away from the root note.

●It can either be a major or minor 3rd interval away from the root note.

●Since this is a minor chord the middle note is a minor 3rd interval away from the root note of our chord.

●The root note of our chord is A.

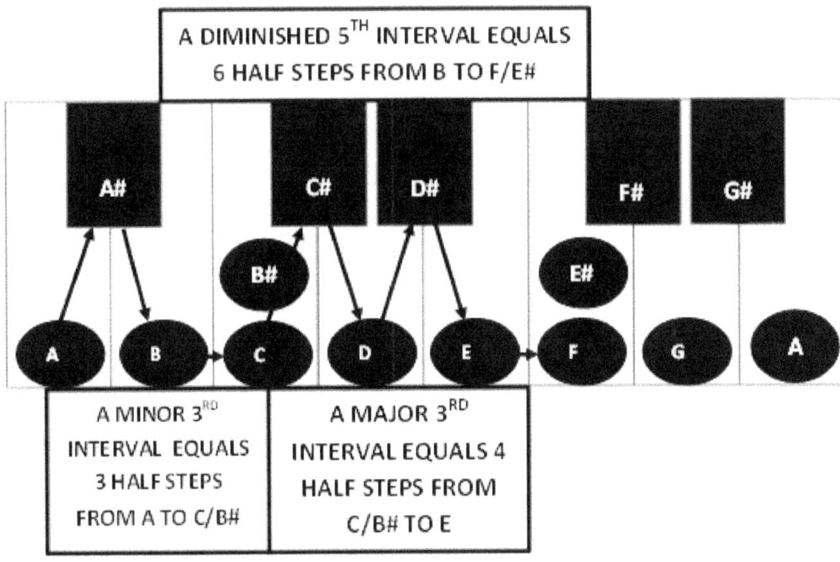

CHORD NUMBER	CHORD NAME	MIDDLE NOTE OR THE 3RD IS A MAJOR OR MINOR 3RD AWAY FROM THE ROOT NOTE.	NOTES
i	A minor	AC	ACE
ii°	B diminished	B??	BDF
III	C major	CE	CEG
iv	D minor	DF	DFA
v	E minor	EG	EGB
VI	F major	FA	FAC
VII	G major	GB	GBD

•The middle note is either a major 3rd or a minor 3rd interval away from the root note.

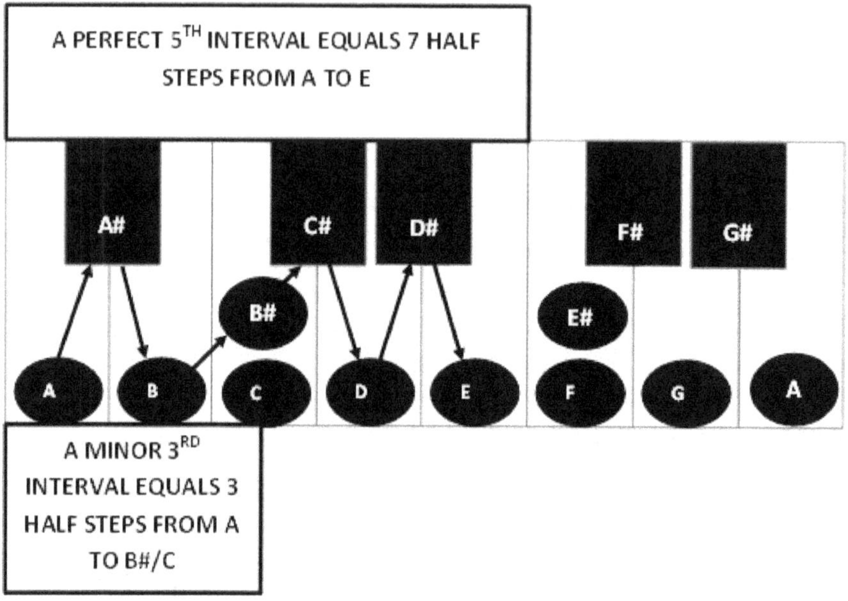

•Now for the B diminished chord the second note has to be a major 3rd interval away from the root note B of our chord. This note is D#.

•The last note is always a perfect 5th interval away from the root note B of our chord. This note is F#.

•We then lower these two notes the 3rd and the 5th by a half step.

•This spells the B diminished chord as BDF.

•The diminished chord is thus formed: Root + minor 3rd + diminished 5th.

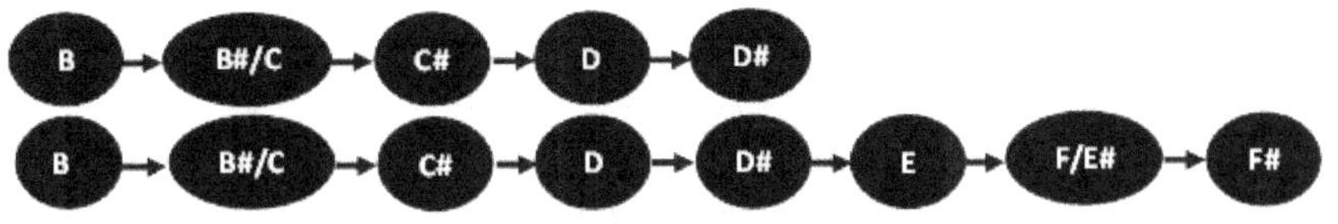

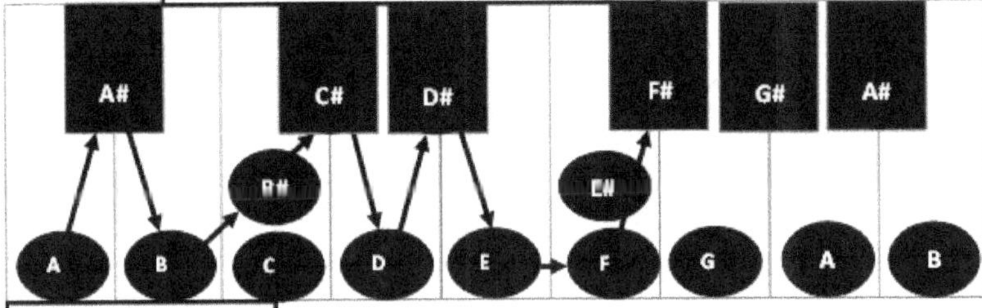

A PERFECT 5TH INTERVAL EQUALS 7 HALF STEPS FROM B TO F#.

A MAJOR 3RD INTERVAL EQUAL 4 HALF STEPS FROM B TO D#

A MINOR 3RD INTERVAL EQUALS 3 HALF STEPS FROM A TO B# /C

FIGURING OUT THE NOTES OF THE TRIAD CHORDS IN A MINOR KEY USING THE MIRROR DIRECTLY

•Just by looking at our mirror we already have the first note which is the root and the last note which is the 5th. All we have to do is to find our middle note.

1. A MINOR CHORD A?E

•To find the middle note or a minor 3rd interval away from A.

•We will start counting at A and go up 5 letters to the right landing on C#.

•This is going up in perfect 5ths intervals which is equal to 7 half steps from letter to letter on the mirror.

•Now since this is minor chord, we will lower the C# by a half step to C.

•This effectively spells out the A minor chord as ACE.

2. B DIMINISHED CHORD B??

•How do we find our middle note the 3rd and our last note the 5th?

•Now the middle note or 3rd is a minor 3rd interval away from the root note B.

•The last note which is the 5th is a diminished 5th interval away from the root note B.

•We will start counting at B along line 3 and go up 5 letters to the right landing on D# along line 3.

•Now this is going up in perfect 5ths intervals which is equal to 7 half steps from letter to letter on the mirror.

•Now since this note is a minor 3rd interval away from the root note B we will lower the D# by a half step to D.

•Now for our last note or the 5th we will start counting at B and as usual just by looking at our mirror we already have our first note the root B and our last note the 5th F#.

•So, starting at B we will go up one letter to the right.

•This is going up a perfect 5th interval which is equal to 7 half steps on the key board landing us on F#.

•Now we lower the F# by a half step to F.

•This spells our B diminished chord as BDF.

3. C MAJOR CHORD C?G

•To find our middle note or a major 3rd interval away from C.

•We will start counting at C and go up 5 letters to the right landing on E on line 2.

•This is going up in perfect 5ths intervals which is equal to 7 half steps from letter to letter on the mirror.

•This effectively spells out the C major chord as CEG.

4. D MINOR CHORD D?A

•To find our middle note or a minor 3rd interval away from D.

•We will start counting at D along line 2 and go up 5 letters to the right of landing us on F#.

•This is going up in perfect 5ths intervals which is equal to 7 half steps from letter to letter on the mirror.

•Now since this is a minor chord we will lower the F# by a half step to F.

•So our D minor chord spells us DFA.

5. E MINOR CHORD E?B

•To find our middle note or a minor 3rd interval away from E.

•We will start counting at E on line 3 and go up 5 letters to the right landing on G#.

•This is going up in perfect 5ths intervals which is equal to 7 half steps from letter to letter on the mirror.

•Now since this is a minor chord we will lower the G# by a half step to G.

•So our E minor chord spells us EGB.

6. F MAJOR CHORD F?C

- To find our middle note or a major 3rd interval away from F.

- We will start counting at F on line 3 and go up 5 letters to the right landing on A.

- This is going up in perfect 5ths intervals which is equal to 7 half steps from letter to letter on the mirror.

- This effectively spells out our F major chord as FAC.

7. G MAJOR CHORD G?D

- To find our middle note or a major 3rd interval away from G.

- We will start counting at G on line 2 and go up 5 letters to the right landing on B.

- This is going up in perfect 5ths intervals which is equal to 7 half steps from letter to letter on the mirror.

- This effectively spells out our G major chord as GBD.

FIGURING OUT TYPES OF CHORDS IN THE C♭ MAJOR KEY USING MIRROR

*Let us take C♭ to be:

●A major key.

●Note number 1 or tonic of our C♭ major key/scale.

●The I chord in our C♭ major key/scale.

●The root note of our I chord.

●We need to create the C♭ major scale both on paper and on keyboard. The underlined letters form the major scale and we will follow the pattern used to create any major scale of whole step, whole step, half step, whole step, whole step, whole step, half step.

●Remember now that we are in the flat side of the mirror.

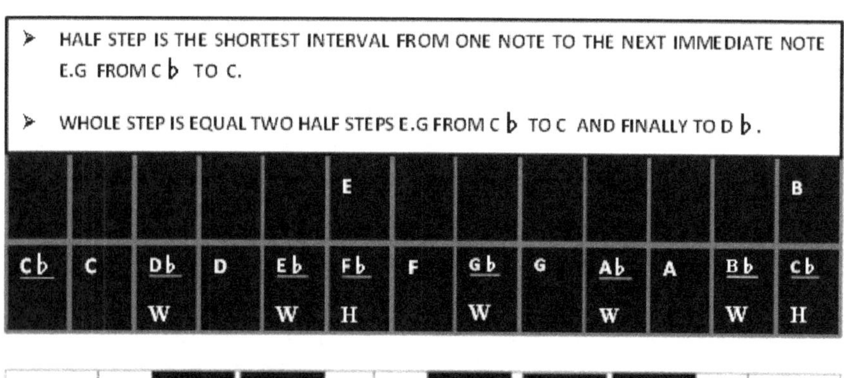

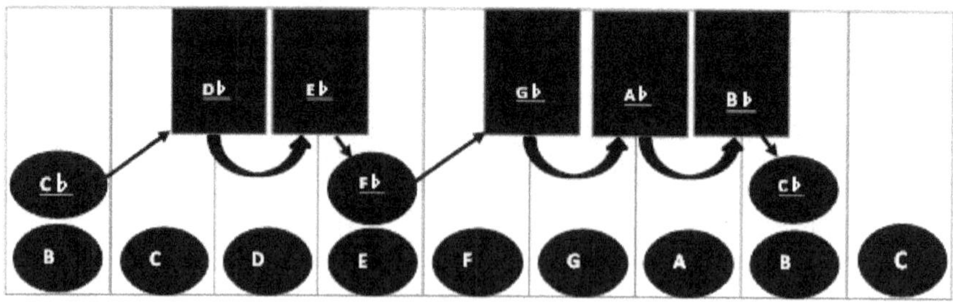

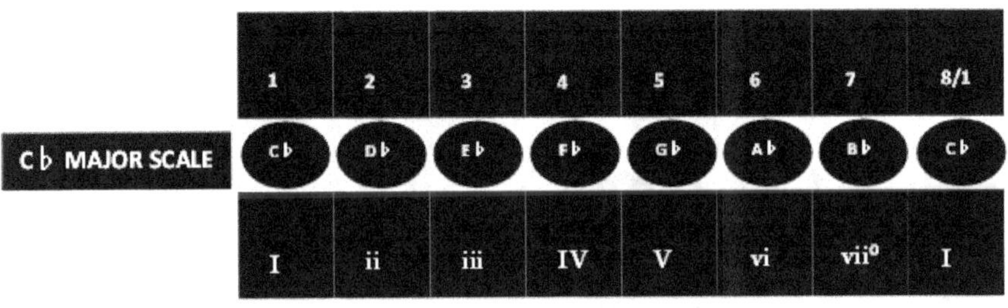

●To know which chords are major, minor or diminished let's look into our mirror.

●Looking at line 1 letters to the left and right of C ♭ are major chords including C ♭ itself.

●Now let us start at C ♭ which is note number one in our C ♭ major key/ scale.

●This is going to be our C ♭ major chord and we are going to designate it the uppercase Roman numeral I.

●To the right of C ♭ we have the note G ♭ which is note number 5 in our C ♭ major scale.

●This is going to be our G ♭ major chord and we are going to designate it the uppercase Roman numeral V.

●Now going up one letter to the right of C ♭ as we have done is going up a perfect 5th interval which is equal to 7 half steps on the keyboard from C ♭ to G ♭ . This is the same as going down a perfect 4th interval on the keyboard which is equal to 5 half steps from C ♭ to G.

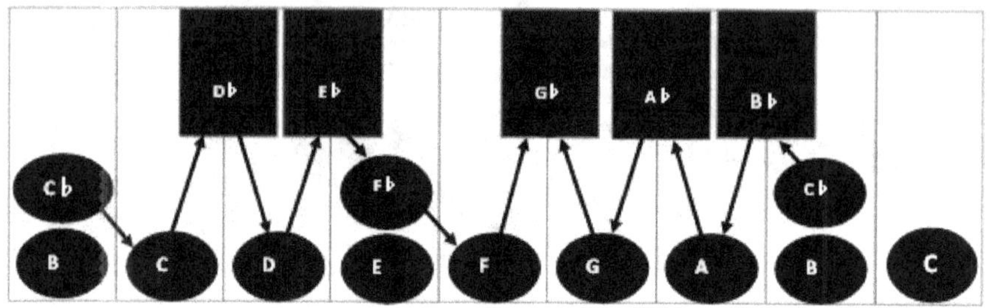

●To the left of C♭ is F♭ which is note number 4 on our C♭ major key/scale. This is going to be our F♭ major chord and we are going to designate it the uppercase Roman numeral IV.

●Now going down one letter to the left of C♭ as we have done here is going down a perfect 5th interval which is equal to 7 half steps from C♭ to F♭ on the keyboard. This is the same as going up a perfect 4th interval which is equal to 5 half steps from C♭ to F♭.

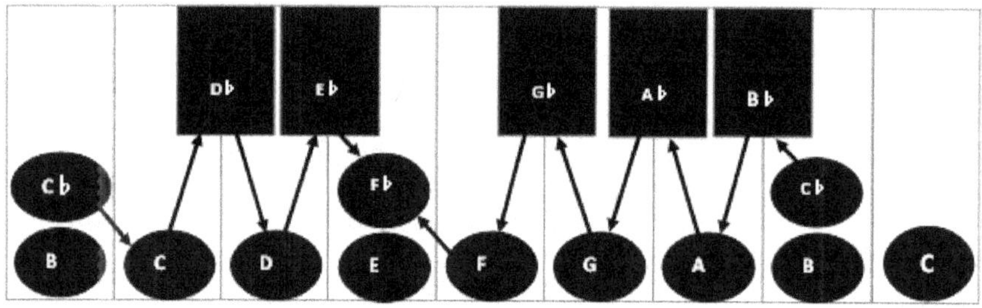

●To know our minor chords from the mirror we will count one letter to the right of G♭ we will land on D♭ one letter to the right of D♭ we land on A♭ and finally one letter to the right of A♭ we land on E♭.

●And we have D♭, A♭, and E♭ as our 3 minor chords.

●Now what we are doing here is that we are going up in perfect 5ths intervals from G♭ to D♭ to A♭ to E♭.

●Now D♭ is note number 2 in our C♭ major scale and we will designate it the lowercase Roman numeral ii.

●Note A♭ is note number 6 in our C♭ major scale and we will designate it the lowercase Roman numeral vi.

●Note E♭ is note number 3 in our C♭ major scale and we will designate it the lowercase Roman numeral iii.

●Finally going one letter up to the right of E♭ you land on B♭ this is going up a perfect 5th interval which is equal to going up 7 half steps from E♭ to B♭ on the keyboard we have the last chord which is B♭ diminished.

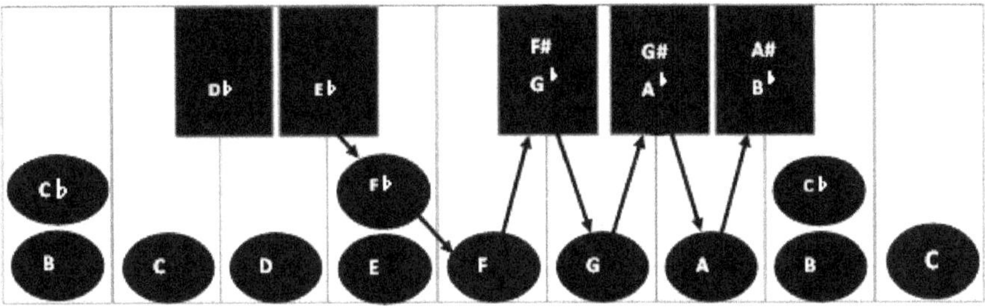

●B♭ is note number 7 in our C♭ major scale.

●So we will designate it the lowercase Roman number vii⁰ with a small circle on top to distinguish it as a diminished chord.

FIGURING OUT THE NOTES OF THE TRIAD CHORDS IN C♭ MAJOR KEY USING THE MIRROR INDIRECTLY

●Let us start with our I chord which is C♭ major chord.

●Looking at our mirror we already have two notes C♭ and G♭.

●The first note C♭ is called the root of the chord.

●The last note G♭ is called the 5th because it's a perfect 5th interval away from the root.

●Now we need to find the middle note which is called the 3rd because it's a 3rd interval away from the root note.

●It can either be a major or minor 3rd interval away from the root note.

●Our root note here is C♭.

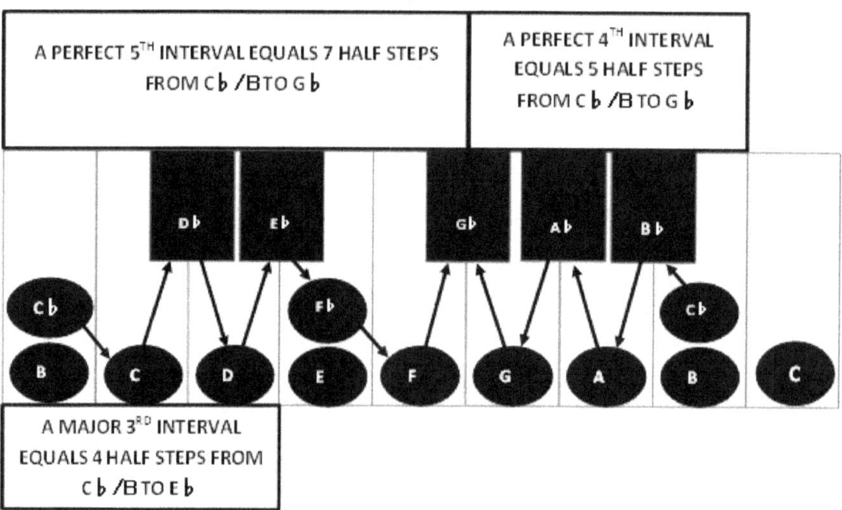

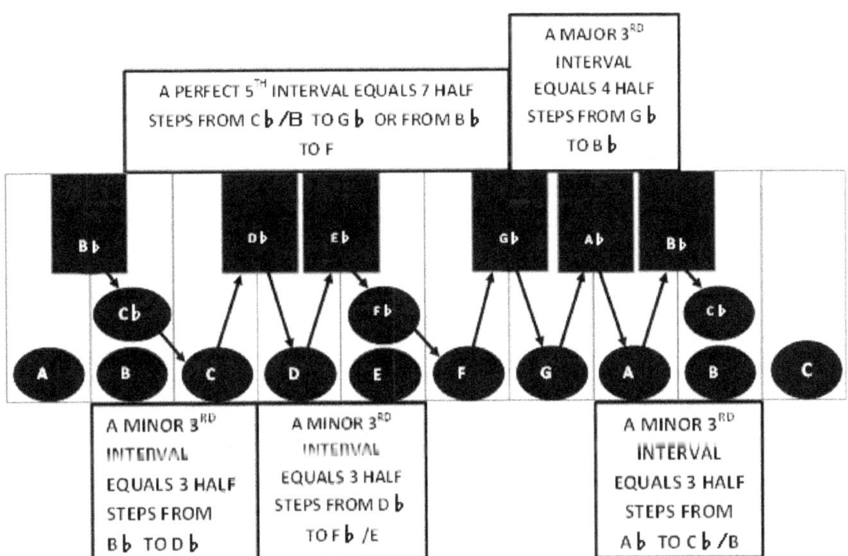

CHORD NUMBER	CHORD NAME	MIDDLE NOTE OR THE 3RD IS A MAJOR OR MINOR 3RD AWAY FROM THE ROOT NOTE.	NOTES
I	C♭ major	C♭E♭	C♭E♭G♭
ii	D♭ minor	D♭F♭	D♭F♭A♭
iii	E♭minor	E♭G♭	E♭G♭B♭
IV	F♭ major	F♭A♭	F♭A♭C♭
V	G♭ major	G♭B♭	G♭B♭D♭
vi	A♭ minor	A♭C♭	A♭C♭E♭
vii°	B♭ diminished	B♭??	B♭D♭F♭

•We shall apply this principle of 3rds intervals for all the other chords in our C♭ major key/scale so as to find out their middle notes.

•Now for the B♭ diminished chord the second note has to be a major 3rd interval away from the root note B♭ of our chord. This note is D.

•The last note is always a perfect 5th interval away from the root note B♭ of our chord. This note is F.

•We then lower these two notes the 3rd and the 5th by a half step.

•This spells the B♭ diminished chord as B♭ D♭ F♭.

●The diminished chord is thus formed: Root + minor 3rd + diminished 5th.

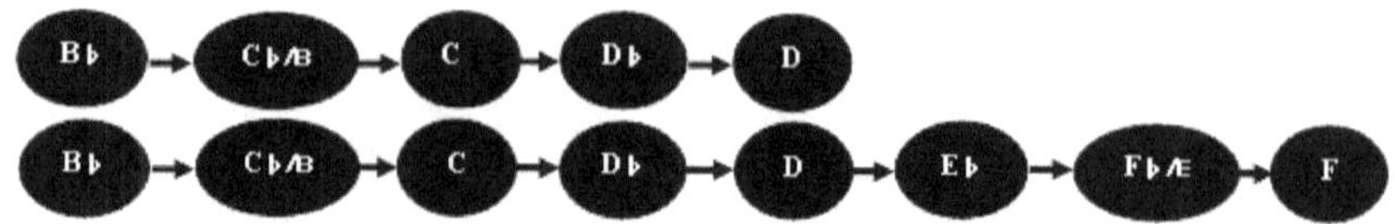

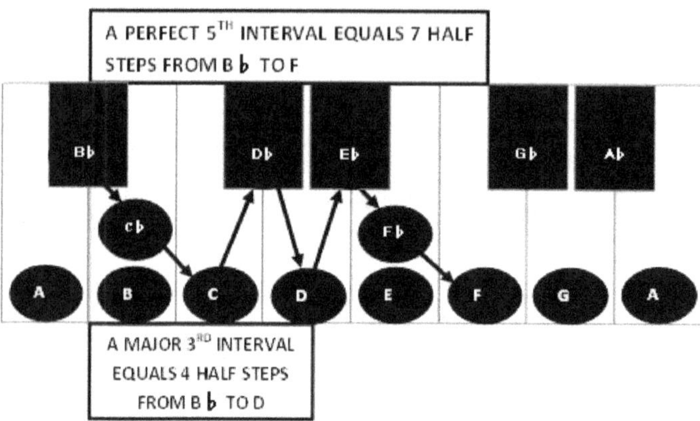

FIGURING OUT THE NOTES OF THE TRIAD CHORDS IN C ♭ MAJOR KEY USING THE MIRROR DIRECTLY

•Just by looking at our mirror we already have the first note which is the root and the last note which is the 5th. All we have to do is to find our middle note.

1. C ♭ MAJOR CHORD C ♭ ? G ♭

•To find the middle note or a major 3rd interval away from C ♭ .

•We will start counting at C ♭ and go up 5 letters to the right landing on   E ♭ .

•This is going up in perfect 5ths intervals which is equal to 7 half steps from letter to letter on the mirror.

•This effectively spells out the C ♭ major chord as C ♭ E ♭ G ♭ .

2. D ♭ MINOR CHORD D ♭ ?A ♭

•To find our middle note or a minor 3rd interval away from D ♭ .

•We will start counting at D ♭ and go up 5 letters to the right landing on F on line 2.

•This is going up in perfect 5ths intervals which is equal to 7 half steps from letter to letter on the mirror.

•Now since this is a minor chord we will lower the F by a half step to F ♭ .

•This effectively spells out the D ♭ minor chord as D ♭ F ♭ A ♭ .

3. E♭ MINOR CHORD E♭ ?B♭

• To find our middle note or a minor 3rd interval away from E♭.

• We will start counting at E♭ and go up 5 letters to the right landing on G along line 3.

• This is going up in perfect 5ths intervals which is equal to 7 half steps from letter to letter on the mirror.

• Now since this is a minor chord we will lower the G by a half step to G♭.

• This effectively spells out the E♭ minor chord as E♭ G♭ B♭.

4. F♭ MAJOR CHORD F♭ ? C♭

• To find our middle note or a major 3rd interval away from F♭.

• We will start counting at F♭ along line 1 and go up 5 letters to the right of F♭ landing us on A♭.

• This is going up in perfect 5ths intervals which is equal to 7 half steps from letter to letter on the mirror.

• So our F♭ major chord spells us F♭ A♭ C♭.

5. G ♭ MAJOR CHORD G ♭ ?D ♭

•To find our middle note or a major 3rd interval away from G ♭ .

•We will start counting at G ♭ along line 1or 2 and go up 5 letters to the right landing on B ♭ .

•This is going up in perfect 5ths intervals which is equal to 7 half steps from letter to letter on the mirror.

•So our G ♭ major chord spells us G ♭ B ♭ D ♭ .

6. A ♭ MINOR CHORD A ♭ ? E ♭

•To find our middle note or a minor 3rd interval away from A ♭ .

•We will start counting at A ♭ along line 3 and go up 5 letters to the right landing on C.

•This is going up in perfect 5ths intervals which is equal to 7 half steps from letter to letter on the mirror.

•Now since this is a minor chord we will lower the C by a half step to C ♭ .

•This effectively spells out our A ♭ minor chord as A ♭ C ♭ E ♭ .

7. B♭ DIMINISHED CHORD B♭ ??

●How do we find our middle note the 3rd and our last note the 5th?

●Now the middle note or 3rd is a minor 3rd interval away from the root note B♭.

●The last note which is the 5th is a diminished 5th interval away from the root note B♭.

●We will start counting at B♭ along line 3 and go up 5 letters to the right landing on D.

●Now this is going up in perfect 5ths intervals which is equal to 7 half steps from letter to letter on the mirror.

●Now since this note is a minor 3rd interval away from the root note B♭ we will lower the D by a half step to D♭.

●Now for our last note or the 5th we will start counting at B♭ and as usual just by looking at our mirror we already have our first note the root B♭ and our last note the 5th F.

●So starting at B♭ we will go up one letter to the right.

●This is going up a perfect 5th interval which is equal to 7 half steps landing us on F.

●Now we lower the F by a half step to F♭.

●This spells our B♭ diminished chord as B♭ D♭ F♭.

FIGURING OUT TYPES OF CHORDS IN THE E MAJOR KEY USING MIRROR

*Let us take E to be:

●A major key.

●Note number 1 or tonic of our E major key/scale.

●The I chord in our E major key/scale.

●The root note of our I chord.

●We need to create the E major scale both on paper and on keyboard. The underlined letters form the major scale and we will follow the pattern used to create any major scale of whole step, whole step, half step, whole step, whole step, whole step, half step.

●Remember we are on the sharp side of our mirror.

> HALF STEP IS THE SHORTEST INTERVAL FROM ONE NOTE TO THE NEXT IMMEDIATE NOTE E.G FROM E TO F /E#. F AND E# ARE ENHARMONIC NOTES ON THE KEYBOARD.
>
> WHOLE STEP IS EQUAL TWO HALF STEPS E.G FROM E TO F /E# AND FINALLY TO F #.

E	F	F#	G	G#	A	A#	B	C	C#	D	D#	E
		W		W	H		W		W		W	H

(E# above F; B# above C)

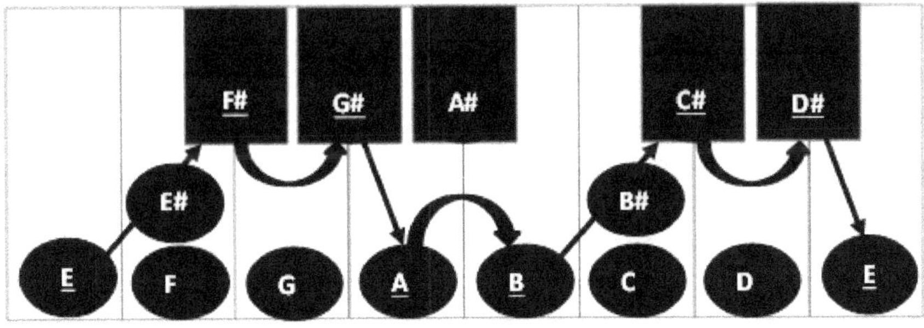

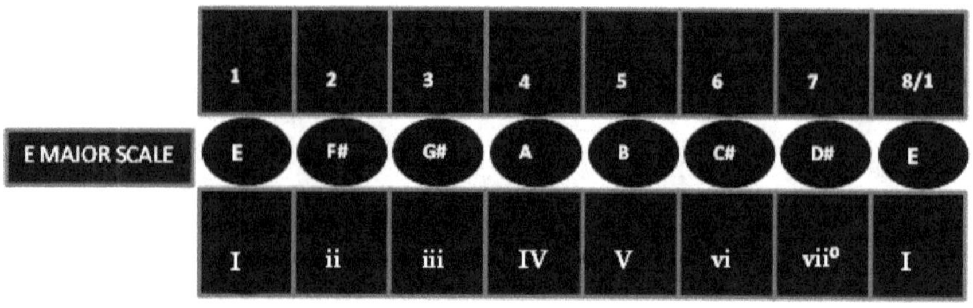

●To know which chords are major, minor or diminished let's look into our mirror.

●Looking at line 2 letters to the left and right of E are major chords including E itself.

●Now let us start at E which is note number one in our E major key/ scale.

●This is going to be our E major chord and we are going to designate it the uppercase Roman numeral I.

●To the right of E we have the note B which is note number 5 in our E major scale.

●This is going to be our B major chord and we are going to designate it the uppercase Roman numeral V.

●Now going up one letter to the right of E as we have done is going up a perfect 5th interval, this is the same as going down a perfect 4th interval.

●To the left of E is A which is note number 4 on our E major key/scale. This is going to be our A major chord and we are going to designate it the uppercase Roman numeral IV.

●Now going down one letter to the left of E as we have done here is going down a perfect 5th interval, this is the same as going up a perfect 4th interval.

●To know our minor chords from the mirror we will count one letter to the right of B we will land on F# one letter to the right of F# we land on C# and finally one letter to the right of C# is G#.

●And we have F#, C# and G# as our 3 minor chords.

●Now what we are doing here is that we are going up in perfect 5ths intervals from B to F# to C# to G#.

●Now F# is note number 2 in our E major scale and we will designate it the lowercase Roman numeral ii.

●Note C# is note number 6 in our E major scale and we will designate it the lowercase Roman numeral vi.

●Note G# is note number 3 in our E major scale and we will designate it the lowercase Roman numeral iii.

●Finally going up one letter to the right of G# which is going up a perfect 5th interval we have the last chord which is D# diminished.

●D# is note number 7 in our E major scale.

●So, we will designate it the lowercase Roman number vii° with a small circle on top to distinguish it as a diminished chord.

FIGURING OUT THE NOTES OF THE TRIAD CHORDS IN E MAJOR KEY USING THE MIRROR INDIRECTLY

•Let us start with our I chord which is E major chord.

•Looking at our mirror we already have two notes E and B.

•The first note E is called the root of the chord.

•The last note B is called the 5th because it's a perfect 5th interval away from the root note.

•Now we need to find the middle note which is called the 3rd because it's a 3rd interval away from the root note.

•The middle note is either a major 3rd or a minor 3rd interval away from the root note.

•Our root note here is E.

•We shall apply this principle of 3rds intervals for all the other chords in our E major key/scale so as to find out all their middle notes.

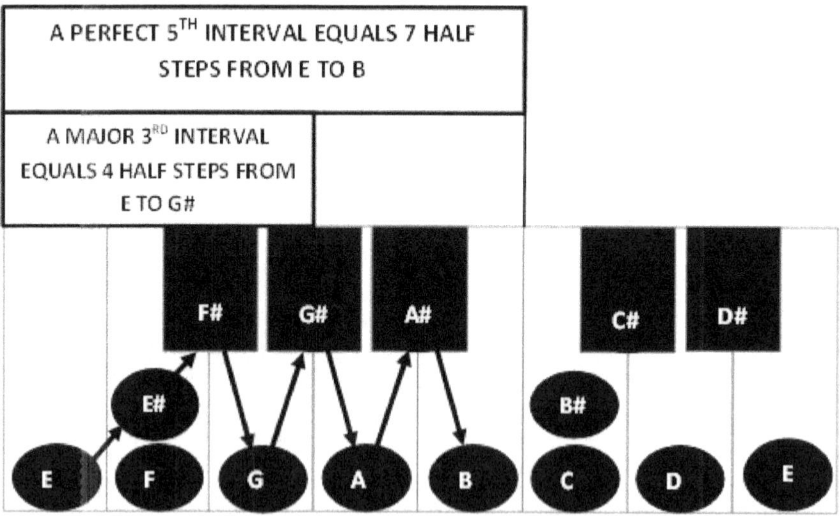

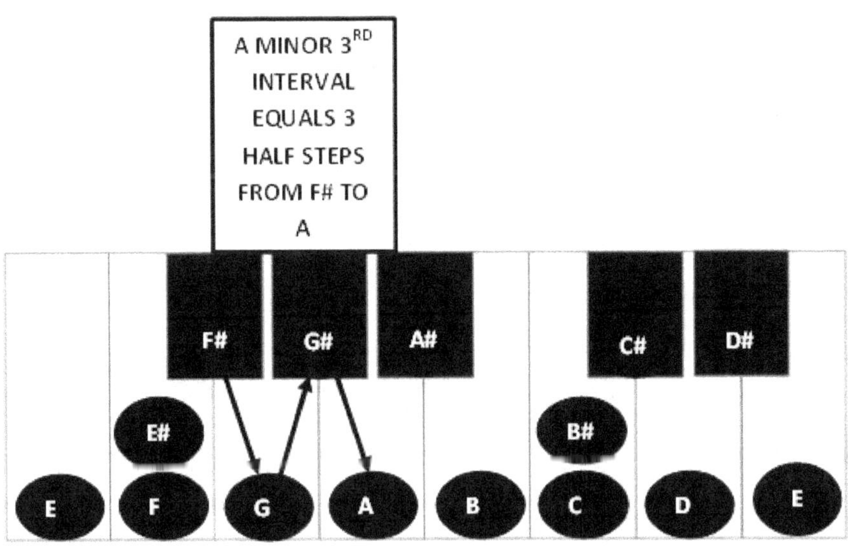

CHORD NUMBER	CHORD NAME	MIDDLE NOTE OR THE 3RD IS A MAJOR OR MINOR 3RD AWAY FROM THE ROOT NOTE.	NOTES
I	E major	EG#	EG#B
ii	F# minor	F#A	F#AC#
iii	G # minor	G#B	G#BD#
IV	A major	AC#	AC#E
V	B major	BD#	BD#F#
vi	C# minor	C#E	C#EG#
vii⁰	D# diminished	D#??	D#F#A

●Now for the D# diminished chord the second note has to be a major 3rd interval away from the root note D# of our chord. This note is G.

●The last note is always a perfect 5th interval away from the root note D# of our chord. This note is A#.

●We then lower these two notes the 3rd and the 5th by a half step.

●This spells the D# diminished chord as D#F#A.

●The diminished chord is thus formed: Root + minor 3rd + diminished 5th.

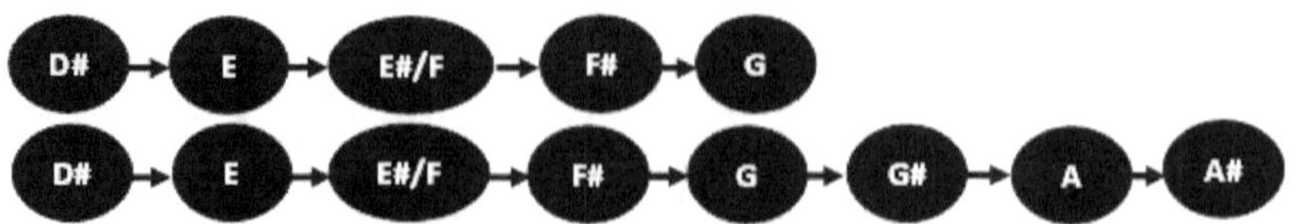

D# → E → E#/F → F# → G
D# → E → E#/F → F# → G → G# → A → A#

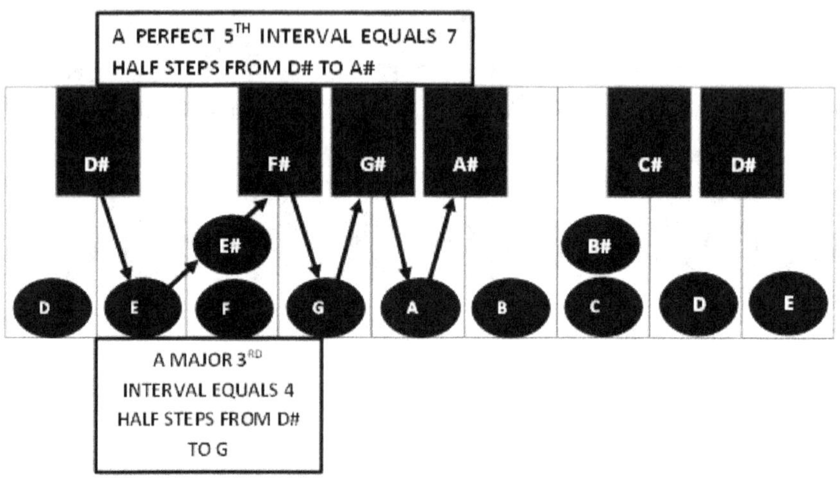

A PERFECT 5TH INTERVAL EQUALS 7 HALF STEPS FROM D# TO A#
D#
F#
G#
A#
C#
D#
E#
B#
D
E
F
G
A
B
C
D
E
A MAJOR 3RD INTERVAL EQUALS 4 HALF STEPS FROM D# TO G

FIGURING OUT THE NOTES OF THE TRIAD CHORDS IN E MAJOR KEY USING THE MIRROR DIRECTLY

1. E MAJOR CHORD E?B

●To find the middle note or a major 3rd interval away from E.

●We will start counting at E and go up 5 letters to the right landing on G#.

●This is going up in perfect 5ths intervals from letter to letter on the mirror.

●This effectively spells out the E major chord as EG#B.

2. F# MINOR CHORD F#?C#

●To find our middle note or a minor 3rd interval away from F#.

●We will start counting at F# and go up 5 letters to the right landing on A# either on line 1 or 3.

●This is going up in perfect 5ths intervals.

●Now since this is a minor chord we will lower the A# by a half step to A.

●This effectively spells out the F# minor chord as F#AC#.

3. G# MINOR CHORD G#?D#

●To find our middle note or a minor 3rd interval away from G#.

•We will start counting at G # and go up 5 letters to the right landing on B#.

•This is going up in perfect 5ths intervals.

•Now since this is a minor chord we will lower the B# by a half step to B.

•This effectively spells out the G# minor chord as G#BD#.

4. A MAJOR CHORD A?E

•To find our middle note or a major 3rd interval away from A.

•We will start counting at A and go up 5 letters to the right of A landing us on C#.

•You can start counting from A either on line 2 or 3 which still lands you on C#.

•This is going up in perfect 5ths intervals from letter to letter on the mirror.

•So our A major chord spells us AC#E.

5. B MAJOR CHORD B?F#

•To find our middle note or a major 3rd interval away from B.

•We will start counting at B and go up 5 letters to the right landing on D# on line 3.

•This is going up in perfect 5ths intervals from letter to letter on the mirror.

●So, our B major chord spells us BD#F#.

6. C# MINOR CHORD C#?G#

●To find our middle note or a minor 3rd interval away from C#.

●We will start counting at C# and go up 5 letters to the right landing on E# on line 1.

●This is going up in perfect 5ths intervals.

●Now since this is a minor chord we will lower the E# by a half step to E.

●This effectively spells out our C# minor chord as C#EG#.

7. D# DIMINISHED CHORD D#??

●How do we find our middle note the 3rd and our last note the 5th?

●Now the middle note or 3rd is a minor 3rd interval away from the root note D#.

●The last note which is the 5th is a diminished 5th interval away from root note D#.

●We will start counting at D# along line 1 and go up 5 letters to the right landing on G along line 2.

●Now this is going up in perfect 5ths intervals from letter to letter on the mirror.

•Now since this note is a minor 3rd interval away from the root note D# we will lower the G by a half step to F#.

•Now you may wonder how we got to G when counting up in perfect fifths intervals and then lowering it by a half step to F#.

•This is because B# and C are enharmonic notes and are actually one and the same note on the keyboard, and so when we are counting up 5 letters starting at D# we will treat C as B# to get to G.

•Now for our last note or the 5th we will start counting at D# and as usual just by looking at our mirror we already have our first note the root D# and our last note the 5th A#.

•So, starting at D# we will go up one letter to the right.

•This is going up a perfect 5th interval landing on A#.

•Now we lower the A# by a half step to A.

•This spells our D# diminished chord as D#F#A.

FIGURING OUT TYPES OF CHORDS IN B MAJOR KEY USING THE MIRROR

*Let us take B to be:

- A major key.

- Note number 1 or tonic of our B major key/scale.

- The I chord in our B major key/scale.

- The root note of our I chord.

- We need to create the B major scale both on paper and on keyboard.

- Remember we are on the sharp side of our mirror.

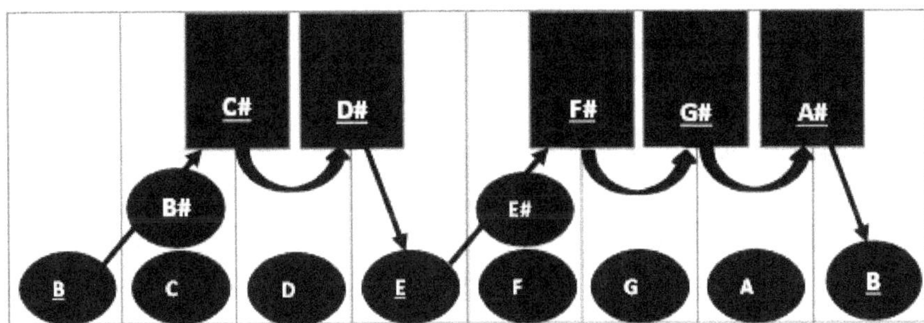

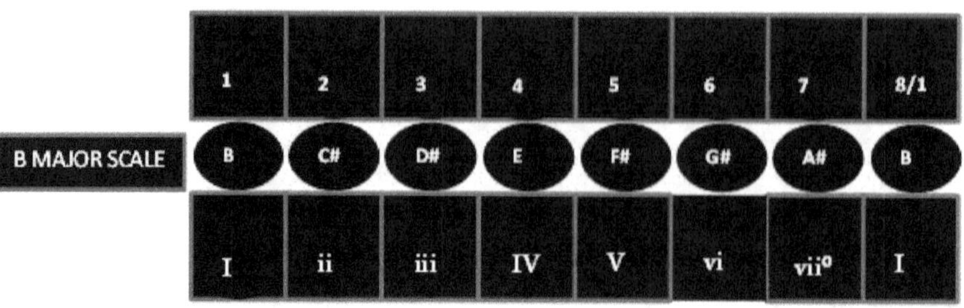

●To know which chords are major, minor or diminished let's look into our mirror.

●Looking at line 2 letters to the left and right of B are major chords including B itself.

●Now let us start at B which is note number one in our B major key/scale.

●This is going to be our B major chord and we are going to designate it the uppercase Roman numeral I.

●To the right of B we have the note F# which is note number 5 in our B major scale.

●This is going to be our F# major chord and we are going to designate it the uppercase Roman numeral V.

●Going up one letter to the right of B as we have done is going up a perfect 5th interval, this is the same as going down a perfect 4th interval.

●To the left of B is the note E which is note number 4 on our B major key/scale.

●This is going to be our E major chord and we are going to designate it the uppercase Roman numeral IV.

●Now going down one letter to the left of B as we have done here is going down a perfect 5th interval, this is the same as going up a perfect 4th interval.

•To know our 3 minor chords from the mirror we will move one letter to the right of F# we will land on C# one letter to the right of C# we land on G# and finally one letter to the right of G# We land on D#.

•And we have C# G# and D# as our 3 minor chords.

•Now what we are doing here is that we are going up in perfect 5ths intervals from F# to C# to G# to D#.

•We could also go down in perfect 5ths intervals from D# to G# to C# to F#.

•Now C# is note number 2 in our B major scale and we will designate it the lowercase Roman numeral ii.

•Note G# is note number 6 in our B major scale and we will designate it the lowercase Roman numeral vi.

•Note D# is note number 3 in our B major scale and we will designate it the lowercase Roman numeral iii.

•Finally going one letter up from D# or going up a perfect 5th interval from D# we have our last chord which is A# diminished.

•A# is note number 7 in our B major scale.

•So we designate it the lowercase Roman numeral vii^{0} with the small circle on top to distinguish it as a diminished chord.

FIGURING OUT THE NOTES OF THE TRIAD CHORDS IN B MAJOR KEY USING THE MIRROR INDIRECTLY

•Let us start with our I chord which is B major chord.

•Looking at our mirror we already have two notes B and F#.

•The first note B is called the root of the chord.

•The last note F# is called the 5th because it's a perfect 5th interval away from the root note.

•Now we need to find the middle note which is called the 3rd because it's a 3rd interval away from the root note.

•Our root note here is B.

•Now the middle note is either a major 3rd or a minor 3rd interval away from the root note.

•We shall apply this principle of 3rds intervals for all the other chords in the B major scale/key so as to find out their middle notes.

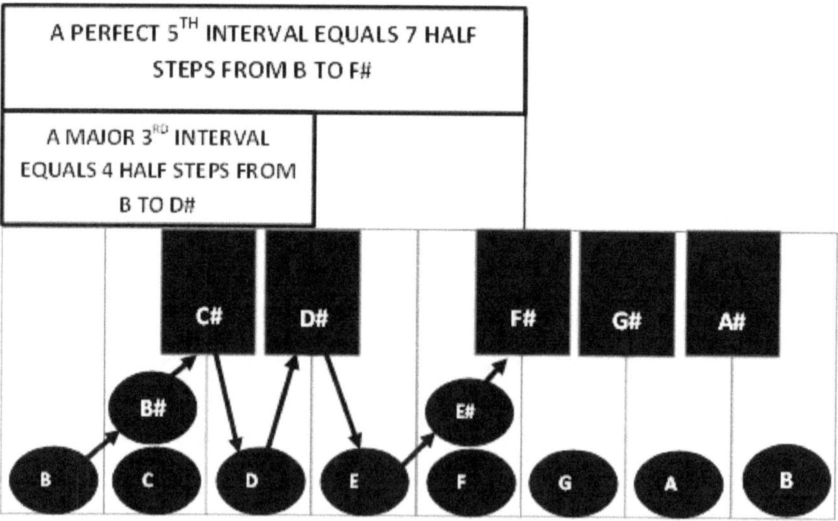

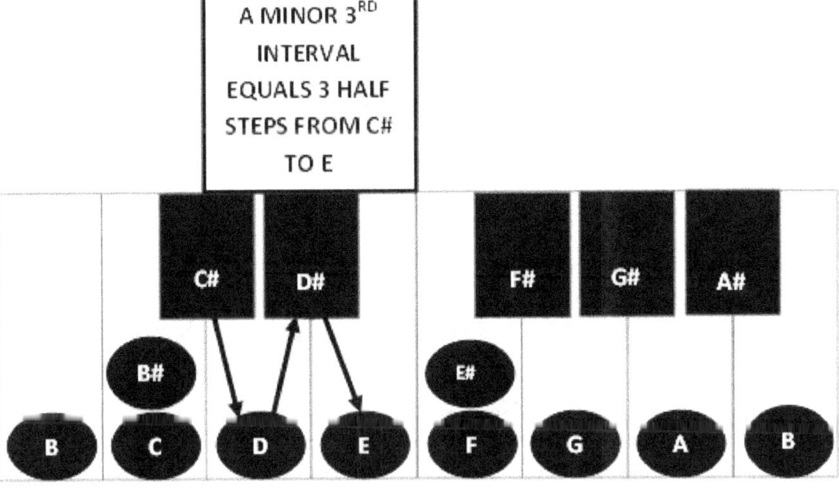

CHORD NUMBER	CHORD NAME	MIDDLE NOTE OR THE 3RD IS A MAJOR OR MINOR 3RD AWAY FROM THE ROOT NOTE.	NOTES
I	B major	BD#	BD#F#
ii	C# minor	C#E	C#EG#
iii	D # minor	D#F#	D#F#A#
IV	E major	EG#	EG#B
V	F# major	F#A#	F#A#C#
vi	G# minor	G#B	G#BD#
vii°	A# diminished	A#??	A#C#E

●Now for the A# diminished chord the second note has to be a major 3rd interval away from the root note A# of our chord. This note is D.

●The last note is always a perfect 5th interval away from the root note A# of our chord. This note is E#/ F.

●We then lower these two notes the 3rd and the 5th by a half step.

●This spells the A# diminished chord as A#C#E.

●The diminished chord is thus formed: Root + minor 3rd + diminished 5th.

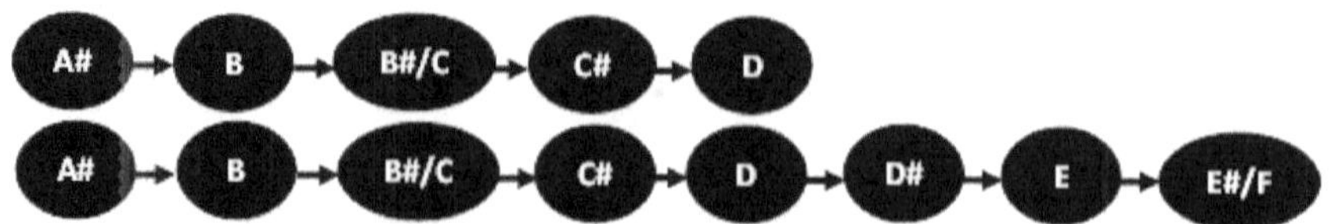

A# → B → B#/C → C# → D
A# → B → B#/C → C# → D → D# → E → E#/F

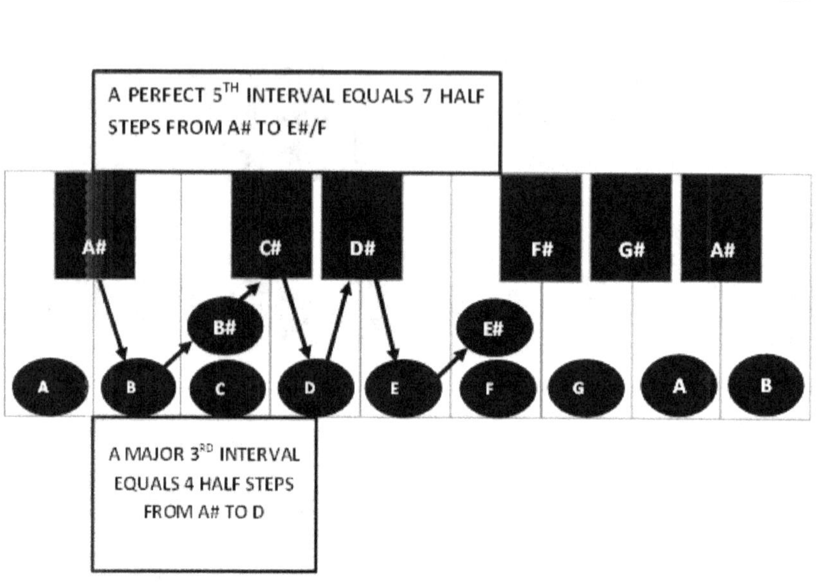

A PERFECT 5TH INTERVAL EQUALS 7 HALF STEPS FROM A# TO E#/F
A#
C#
D#
F#
G#
A#
B#
E#
A
B
C
D
E
F
G
A
B
A MAJOR 3RD INTERVAL EQUALS 4 HALF STEPS FROM A# TO D

FIGURING OUT THE NOTES OF THE TRIAD CHORDS IN B MAJOR KEY USING THE MIRROR DIRECTLY

1. B MAJOR CHORD B?F#

●To find the middle note or a major 3rd interval away from B.

●We will start counting at B along line 3 and go up 5 letters to the right landing on D#.

●This is going up in perfect 5ths intervals from letter to letter on the mirror.

●Our B major chord is spelled as BD#F#.

2. C# MINOR CHORD C#?G#

●To find our middle note or a minor 3rd interval away from C#.

●We will start counting at C# on line 1 and go up 5 letters to the right landing on E#.

●This is going up in perfect 5ths intervals.

●Now since this is a minor chord we will lower the E# by a half step to E.

●This effectively spells out the C# minor chord as C#EG#.

3. D# MINOR CHORD D#?A#

●To find our middle note or a minor 3rd interval away from D#.

●We will start counting at D # on line 1 and go up 5 letters to the right landing on G.

●Remember B# and C are enharmonic notes so we treat C as B# to get to G.

●This is going up in perfect 5ths intervals.

●Now since this is a minor chord we will lower the G by a half step to F#.

●This effectively spells out the D# minor chord as D#F#A#.

4. E MAJOR CHORD E?B

●To find our middle note or a major 3rd interval away from E.

●We will start counting at E along line 3 and go up 5 letters to the right landing us on G#.

●This is going up in perfect 5ths intervals from letter to letter on the mirror.

●So, our E major chord spells us EG#B.

5. F# MAJOR CHORD F#?C#

•To find our middle note or a major 3rd interval away from F#.

•We will start counting at F# and go up 5 letters to the right landing on A#.

•You can start counting either from line 1 or 3.

•This is going up in perfect 5ths intervals from letter to letter on the mirror.

•So, our F# major chord is spelled as F#A#C#.

6. G# MINOR CHORD G#?D#

•To find our middle note or a minor 3rd interval away from G#.

•We will start counting at G# along line 1 and go up 5 letters to the right landing on B#.

•This is going up in perfect 5ths intervals from letter to letter on the mirror.

•Now since this is a minor chord we will lower the B# by a half step to B.

•This effectively spells out our G# minor chord as G#BD#.

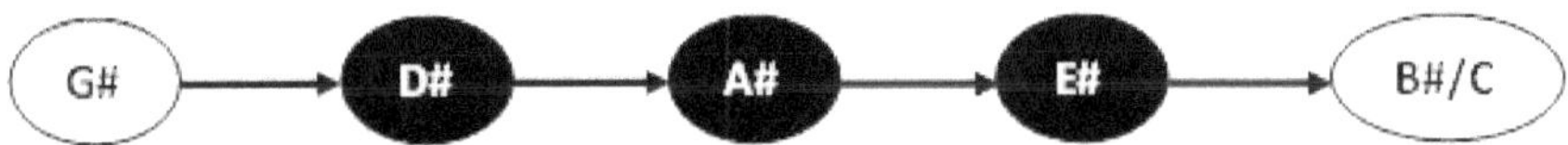

7. A# DIMINISHED CHORD A#??

•How do we find our middle note the 3rd and our last note the 5th?

•Now the middle note or 3rd is a minor 3rd interval away from the root note A#.

•The last note which is the 5th is a diminished 5th interval away from A# the root note.

•We will start counting at A# along line 1 and go up 5 letters to the right landing on D along line 2.

•Now this is going up in perfect 5ths intervals from letter to letter on the mirror.

•Now since this note is a minor 3rd interval away from the root note A# we will lower the D by a half step to C#.

•Now you may wonder how we got to D when counting up in perfect fifths intervals and then lowering it by a half step to C#.

•This is because B# and C are enharmonic notes and are actually one and the same note on the keyboard and so when we are counting up 5 letters starting at A# we will go to E# and then treat C as B# to get to G and finally D.

•Now for our last note or the 5th we will start counting at A# and as usual just by looking at our mirror we already have our first note the root A# and our last note the 5th E#.

•So, starting at A# we will go up one letter to the right.

•This is going up a perfect 5th interval landing us on E#.

•Now we lower the E# by a half step to E.

•This spells our A# diminished chord as A#C#E.

FIGURING OUT TYPES OF CHORDS IN F# MAJOR KEY USING MIRROR

*Let us take F# to be:

- A major key.

- Note number 1 or tonic of our F# major key/scale.

- The I chord in our F# major key/scale.

- The root note of our I chord.

- We need to create the F# major key both on paper and on keyboard.

- Remember we are on the sharp side of our mirror.

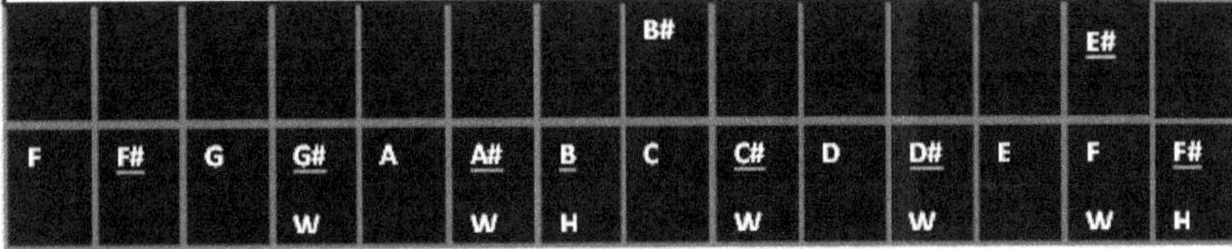

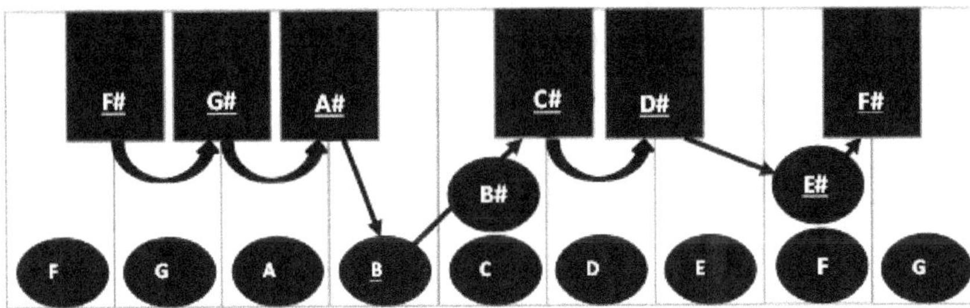

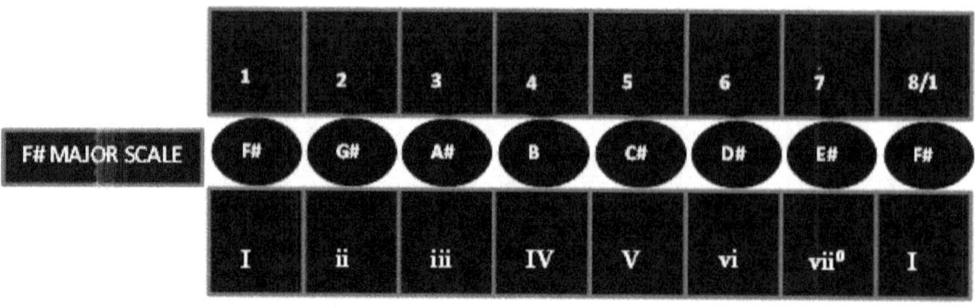

●To know which chords are major, minor or diminished let's look into our mirror.

●Looking at line 2 letters to the left and right of F# are major chords including F# itself.

●Now let us start at F# which is note number one in our F# major key/ scale.

●This is going to be our F# major chord and we are going to designate it the uppercase Roman numeral I.

●To the right of F# we have the note C# which is note number 5 in our F# major scale.

●This is going to be our C# major chord and we are going to designate it the uppercase Roman numeral V.

●Now going up one letter to the right of F# as we have done is going up a perfect 5th interval, this is the same as going down a perfect 4th interval.

●To the left of F# is B which is note number 4 on our F# major key/scale. This is going to be our B major chord and we are going to designate it the uppercase Roman numeral IV.

●Now going down one letter to the left of F# as we have done here is going down a perfect 5th interval, this is the same as going up a perfect 4th interval.

•To know our 3 minor chords from the mirror we will move one letter to the right of C# landing on G# and again we move one letter to the right of G# we land on D# and finally one letter to the right of D# we land on A#.

•And we have G#, D# and A# as our 3 minor chords.

•Now what we are doing here is that we are going up in perfect 5ths intervals from C# to G# to D# and finally A#.

•We could also go down in perfect 5ths intervals from A# to D# to G# to C#.

•Now G# is note number 2 in our F# major scale and we will designate it the lowercase Roman numeral ii.

•Note D# is note number 6 in our F# major scale and we will designate it the lowercase Roman numeral vi.

•Note A# is note number 3 in our F# major scale and we will designate it the lowercase Roman numeral iii.

•Finally going up one letter to the right of A# which is the same as going up a perfect 5th interval which is equal to 7 half steps from A# to E# on the keyboard we have the last chord which is E# diminished.

•E# is note number 7 in our F# major scale.

•So, we will designate it the lowercase Roman numeral vii° with a small circle on top to distinguish it as a diminished chord.

FIGURING OUT THE NOTES OF THE TRIAD CHORDS IN F# MAJOR KEY USING THE MIRROR INDIRECTLY

•Let us start with our I chord which is F# major chord.

•Looking at our mirror we already have two notes F# and C#.

•The first note F# is called the root of the chord.

•The last note C# is called the 5th because it's a perfect 5th interval away from the root note.

•Now we need to find the middle note which is called the 3rd because it's a 3rd interval away from the root note.

•Our root note here is F#.

•Now the middle note is either a major 3rd or a minor 3rd interval away from the root note.

•We shall apply this principle of 3rds intervals for all other chords in the F# major scale so as to find out their middle notes.

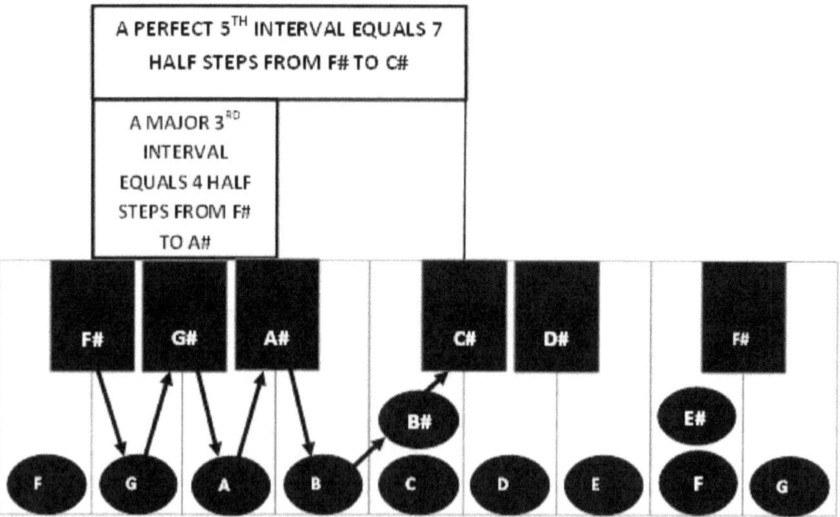

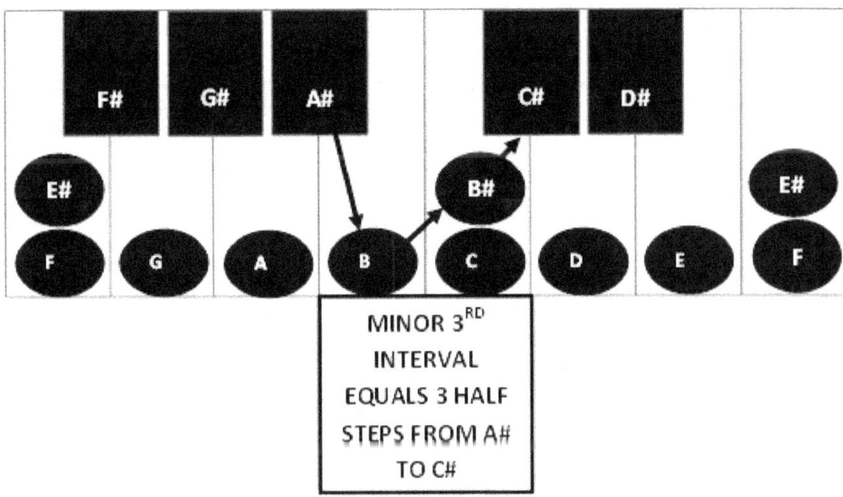

CHORD NUMBER	CHORD NAME	MIDDLE NOTE OR THE 3RD IS A MAJOR OR MINOR 3RD AWAY FROM THE ROOT NOTE.	NOTES
I	F# major	F#A#	F#A#C#
ii	G# minor	G#B	G#BD#
iii	A# minor	A#C#	A#C#E#
IV	B major	BD#	BD#F#
V	C# major	C#E#	C#E#G#
vi	D# minor	D#F#	D#F#A#
vii⁰	E# diminished	E#??	E#G#B

●Now for the E# diminished chord the second note has to be a major 3rd interval away from the root note E# of our chord. This note is A.

●The last note is always a perfect 5th interval away from the root note E# of our chord. This note is B#.

●We then lower these two notes the 3rd and the 5th by a half step.

●This spells the E# diminished chord as E#G#B.

●The diminished chord is thus formed: Root + minor 3rd + diminished 5th.

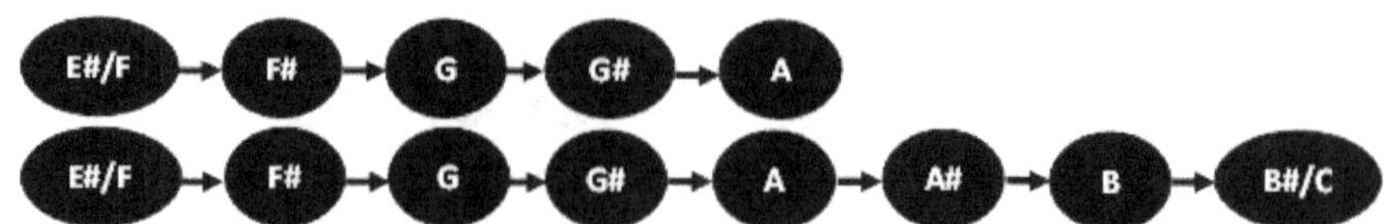

E#/F
F#
G
G#
A
E#/F
F#
G
G#
A
A#
B
B#/C

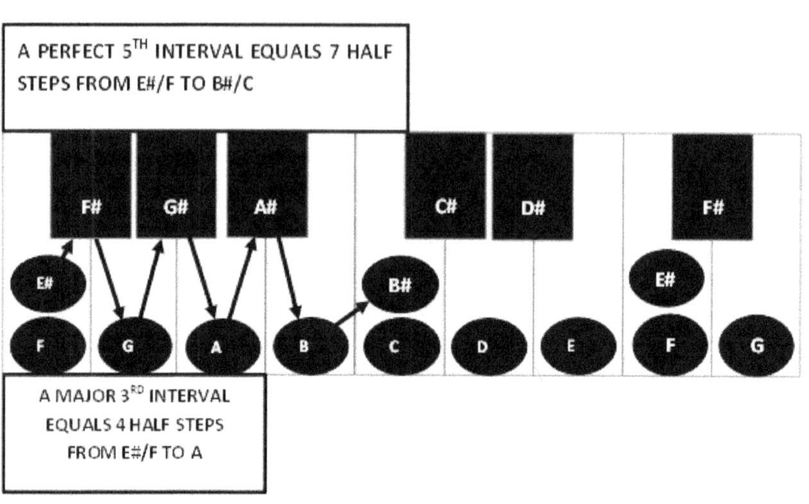

A PERFECT 5TH INTERVAL EQUALS 7 HALF STEPS FROM E#/F TO B#/C
F#
G#
A#
C#
D#
F#
E#
B#
F
G
A
B
C
D
E
E#
F
G
A MAJOR 3RD INTERVAL EQUALS 4 HALF STEPS FROM E#/F TO A

FIGURING OUT THE NOTES OF THE TRIAD CHORDS IN F# MAJOR KEY USING THE MIRROR DIRECTLY

1. F# MAJOR CHORD F#?C#

●How do we find our middle note or a major 3rd interval away from F#?

●We will start counting at F# and go up 5 letters to the right landing on A# either on line 1 or 3.

●This is going up in perfect 5ths intervals.

●Our F# major chord is spelled as F#A#C#.

2. G# MINOR CHORD G#?D#

●How do we find our middle note or a minor 3rd interval away from G#?

●We will start counting at G# and go up 5 letters to the right landing on B# on line 1.

●This is going up in perfect 5ths intervals from letter to letter on the mirror.

●Now since this is a minor chord we will lower the B# by a half step to B.

●This effectively spells out the G# minor chord as G#BD#.

3. A# MINOR CHORD A#?E#

•How do we find our middle note or a minor 3rd interval away from A#?

•We will start counting at A# and go up 5 letters to the right landing on D.

•This is going up in perfect 5ths intervals from letter to letter on the mirror.

•Now since this is a minor chord we will lower the D by half step to C#.

•This effectively spells out the A# minor chord as A#C#E#.

•Now you may wonder how we got to D when counting up in perfect fifths intervals from letter to letter and then lowering it by a half step to C#.

•This is because B# and C are enharmonic keys.

•And so when we are counting up 5 letters starting at A# we will treat C as B# to get to G and finally to D.

4. B MAJOR CHORD B?F#

•How do we find our middle note or a major 3rd interval away from B?

•We will start counting at B along line 2 and go up 5 letters to the right landing us on D# either line 1 or 3.

•This is going up in perfect 5ths intervals from letter to letter on the mirror.

•So our B major chord spells as BD#F#.

5. C# MAJOR CHORD C#?G#

•How do we find our middle note or a major 3rd interval away from C#?

•We will start counting at C# and go up 5 letters to the right landing on E#, you can start counting at C# either on line 1 or 3 and you will still land on E#.

•This is going up in perfect 5ths intervals from letter to letter on the mirror.

•So our C# major chord is spelled as C#E#G#.

6. D# MINOR CHORD D#?A#

•How do we find our middle note?

•We will start counting at D# along line 1 and go up 5 letters to the right landing on G.

•This is going up in perfect 5ths intervals from letter to letter on the mirror.

•Now since this is a minor chord we will lower the G by a half step to F#.

•D# minor chord now spells as D#F#A#.

•Now you may wonder how we got to G when counting up in perfect fifths intervals before lowering it by a half step to F#.

•This is because B# and C are enharmonic notes/keys on the keyboard.

•And so when we are counting up 5 letters starting at D# we will treat C as B# to get to G.

7. E# DIMINISHED CHORD E#??

•How do we find our middle note the 3rd and our last note the 5th?

•Now the middle note or 3rd is a minor 3rd interval away from the root note E#.

•The last note is a diminished 5th interval away from the root note E#.

•We will start counting at E# along line 1 and go up 5 letters to the right landing on A. This is going up in perfect 5ths intervals from letter to letter on the mirror.

•Now since this note is minor 3rd interval away from the root note E# we will lower the A by a half step to G#.

•Now you may wonder how we got to A when counting up in perfect fifths intervals before lowering it by a half step to G#.

•This is because B# and C are enharmonic keys.

•And so when we are counting up 5 letters starting at E# we will treat C as B# to get to G to get to D and finally A.

•For our last note we will start counting at E# and go up one letter to the right.

•This is going up a perfect 5th interval landing on B#.

•So now we lower the B# by a half step B.

•Now we can spell our E# diminished chord as E#G#B.

FIGURING OUT TYPES OF CHORDS IN C# MAJOR KEY USING MIRROR

*Let us take C# to be:

•A major key.

•Note number 1 or tonic of our C# major key/scale.

•The I chord in our C# major key/scale.

•The root note of our I chord.

•We need to create the C# major key both on paper and on keyboard.

•Remember we are on the sharp side of our mirror.

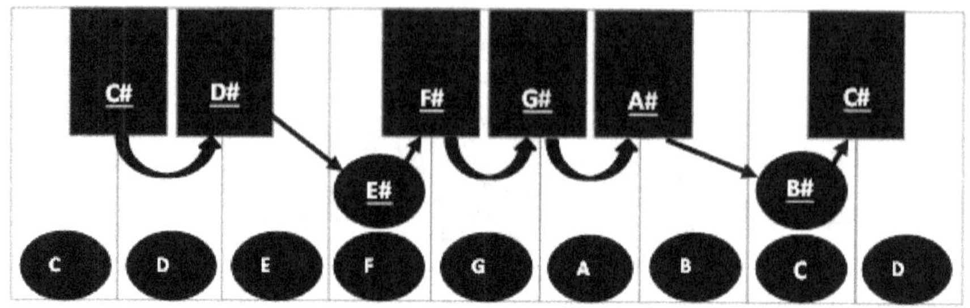

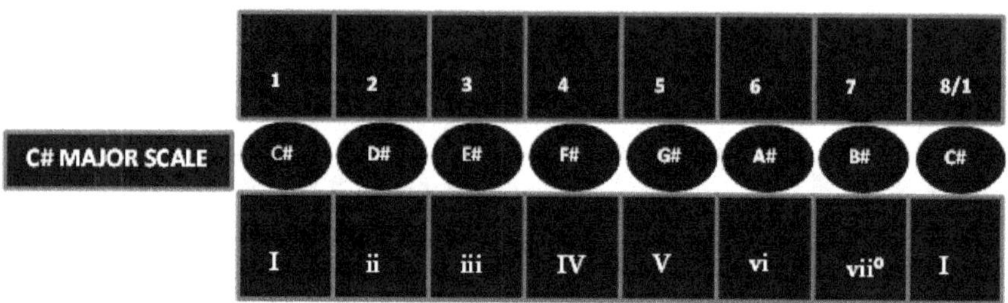

•To know which chords are major, minor or diminished let's look into our mirror.

•Looking at line 1 letters to the left and right of C# are major chords including C# itself.

•Now let us start at C# which is note number one in our C# major key/ scale.

•This is going to be our C# major chord and we are going to designate it the uppercase Roman numeral I.

•To the right of C# we have the note G# which is note number 5 in our C# major scale.

•This is going to be our G# major chord and we are going to designate it the uppercase Roman numeral V.

•Now going up one letter to the right of C# as we have done is going up a perfect 5th interval this is the same as going down a perfect 4th interval.

•To the left of C# is the note F# which is note number 4 in our C# major key/scale.

•This is going to be our F# major chord and we are going to designate it the uppercase Roman numeral IV.

•Now going down one letter to the left of C# as we have done here is going down a perfect 5th interval, this is the same as going up a perfect 4th interval.

•To know our 3 minor chords from the mirror we will move one letter to the right of G# landing on D# and again we move one letter to the right of D# we land on A# and finally one letter to the right of A# we land on E#.

•And we have D#, A# and E# as our 3 minor chords.

•Now what we are doing here is that we are going up in perfect 5ths intervals from G# to D# to A# and finally E#.

•We could also go down in perfect 5ths intervals from E# to A# to D# to G#.

•Now D# is note number 2 in our C# major scale and we will designate it the lowercase Roman numeral ii.

•Note A# is note number 6 in our C# major scale and we will designate it the lowercase Roman numeral vi.

•Note E# is note number 3 in our C# major scale and we will designate it the lowercase Roman numeral iii.

•Finally going up one letter to the right of E# which is the same as going up a perfect 5th interval we have the last chord which is B# diminished.

•B# is note number 7 in our C# major scale.

•So we will designate it the lowercase Roman number vii° with a small circle on top to distinguish it as a diminished chord.

FIGURING OUT THE NOTES OF THE TRIAD CHORDS IN C# MAJOR KEY USING THE MIRROR INDIRECTLY

•Let us start with our I chord which is C# major chord.

•Looking at our mirror we already have two notes C# and G#.

•The first note C# is also called the root note of the chord.

•The last note G# is called the 5th because it's a perfect 5th interval away from the root note.

•Now we need to find the middle note which is called the 3rd because it's a 3rd interval away from the root note.

•Now the middle note is either a major 3rd or a minor 3rd interval away from the root note.

•Our root note here is C#.

•We shall apply this principle of 3rds intervals for all other chords in the C# major key/scale so as to find out their middle notes.

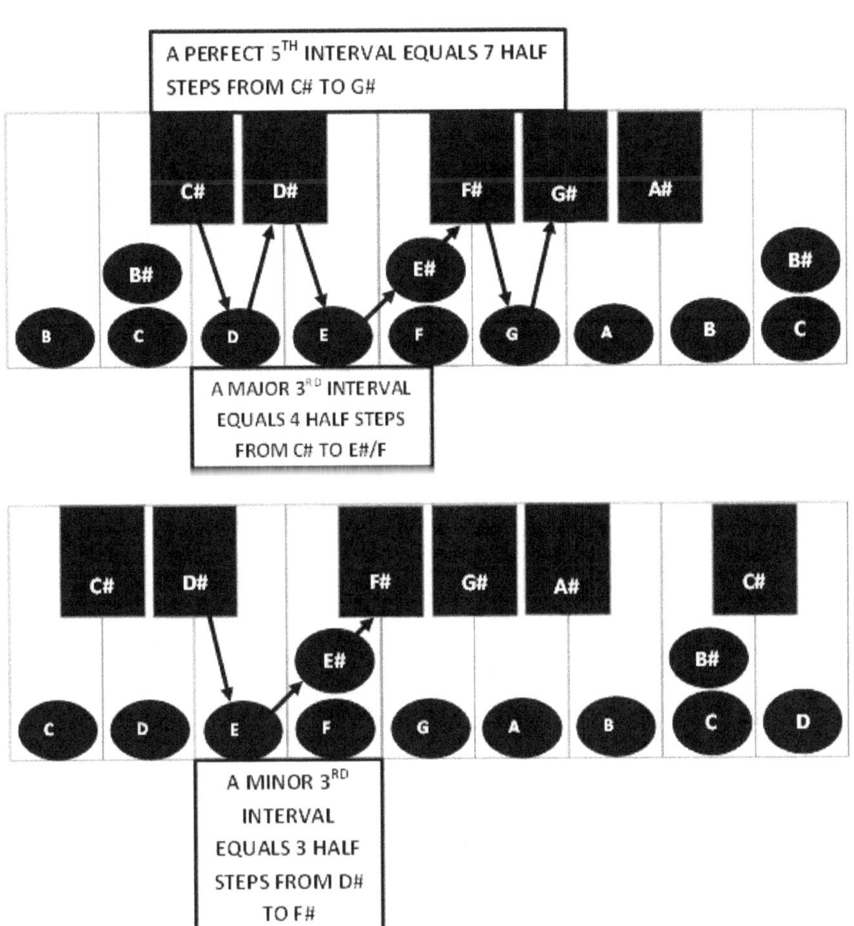

CHORD NUMBER	CHORD NAME	MIDDLE NOTE OR THE 3RD IS A MAJOR OR MINOR 3RD AWAY FROM THE ROOT NOTE.	NOTES
I	C# major	C#E#	C#E#G#
ii	D# minor	D#F#	D#F#A#
iii	E # minor	E#G#	E#G#B#
IV	F# major	F#A#	F#A#C#
V	G# major	G#B#	G#B#D#
vi	A# minor	A#C#	A#C#E#
vii°	B# diminished	B#??	B#D#F#

•Now for the B# diminished chord the 2nd note has to be a major 3rd interval away from B# our root note. This note is E.

•The last note as always is a perfect 5th interval away from B# our root note. This note is G.

●We then lower this two notes the 3rd and the 5th that is the middle and last notes by a half step.

●This spells the B# diminished chord as B#D#F#.

●The diminished chord is thus formed: root + minor 3rd +diminished 5th.

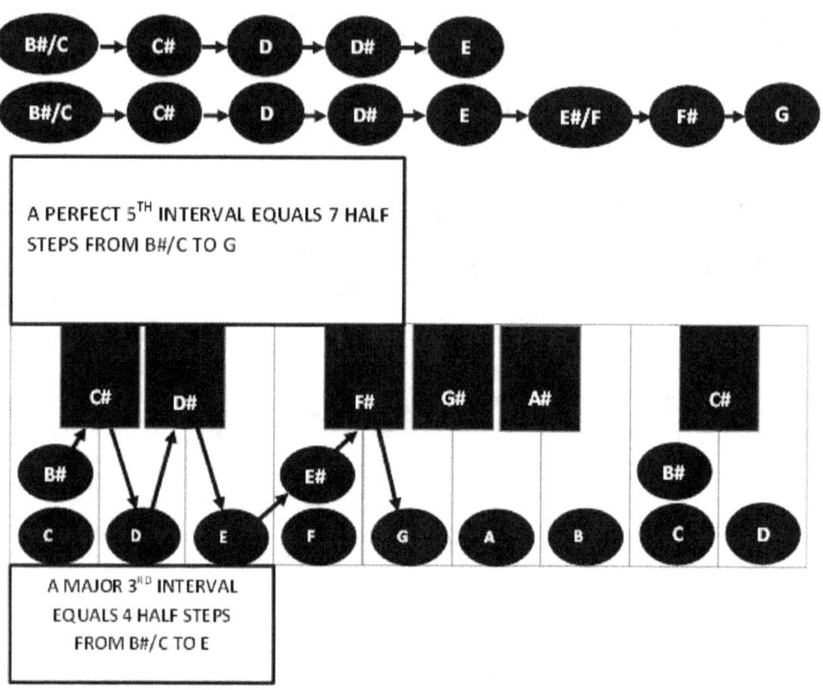

FIGURING OUT THE NOTES OF THE TRIAD CHORDS IN C# MAJOR KEY USING THE MIRROR DIRECTLY

1. C# MAJOR CHORD C#?G#

●How do we find our middle note or a major 3rd interval away from C#?

●We will start counting at C# and go up 5 letters to the right landing on E#.

●This is going up in perfect 5ths intervals.

●Our C# major chord is spelled as C#E#G#.

2. D# MINOR CHORD D#?A#

●How do we find our middle note or a minor 3rd interval away from D#?

●We will start counting at D# and go up 5 letters to the right landing on G on line 2.

●This is going up in perfect 5ths intervals.

●Now since this is a minor chord we will lower the G by a half step to F#.

●This spells out the D# minor chord as D#F#A#.

●Now you may wonder how we got to G when counting up in perfect fifths intervals from letter to letter and then lowering it by a half step to F#.

•This is because B# and C are enharmonic keys/notes on the keyboard and are one and the same.

•And so when we are counting up 5 letters starting at D# we will treat C as B# to get to G.

3. E# MINOR CHORD E#?B#

•How do we find our middle note or a minor 3rd interval away from E#?

•We will start counting at E# and go up 5 letters to the right landing on A.

•Now this is going up in perfect 5ths intervals from letter to letter on the mirror.

•Now since this is a minor chord we will lower the A by half step to G#.

•This effectively spells out the E# minor chord as E#G#B#.

•Now you may wonder how we got to A when counting up in perfect fifths intervals from letter to letter and then lowering it by a half step to G#.

•This is because B# and C are enharmonic keys/notes on the keyboard and they are one and the same, and so when we are counting up 5 letters starting at E# we will treat C as B# to get to G to get to D and finally A.

4. F# MAJOR CHORD F#?C#

●How do we find our middle note or a major 3rd interval away from F#?

●We will start counting at F# either on line 1 or 3 go up 5 letters to the right landing on A#.

●This is going up in perfect 5ths intervals from letter to letter on the mirror.

●So our F# major chord spells as F#A#C#.

5. G# MAJOR CHORD G#?D#

●How do we find our middle note or a major 3rd interval away from G#?

●We will start counting at G# and go up 5 letters to the right landing on B#.

●This is going up in perfect 5ths intervals from letter to letter on the mirror.

●So our G# major chord is spelled as G#B#D#.

6. A# MINOR CHORD A#?E#

●How do we find our middle note or a minor third interval away from A#?

•We will start counting at A# and go up 5 letters to the right landing on D.

•This is going up in perfect 5ths intervals.

•Now since this is a minor chord we will lower the D by a half step to C#.

•So our A# minor chord now spells as A#C#E#.

•Now you may wonder how we got to D when counting up in perfect fifths intervals from letter to letter and then lowering it by a half step to C#.

•This is because B# and C are enharmonic keys/notes.

•And so when we are counting up 5 letters starting at A# we will treat C as B# to get to G and finally D.

7. B# DIMINISHED CHORD B#??

•How do we find our middle note the 3rd and our last note the 5th?

•Now the middle note or 3rd is a minor 3rd interval away from the root note B#.

•The last note which is the 5th is a diminished 5th interval away from the root note B#.

•We will start counting at B# and go up 5 letters to the right landing on E.

•This is going up in perfect 5ths intervals.

•Now since this note is minor 3rd interval away from the root note B# we will lower the E by a half step to D#.

•Now you may wonder how we got to E when counting up in perfect fifths intervals and then lowering it by a half step to D#.

•This is because B# and C are enharmonic keys.

•And so when we are counting up 5 letters we will start counting at C which is actually B# and count up 5 letters landing on E.

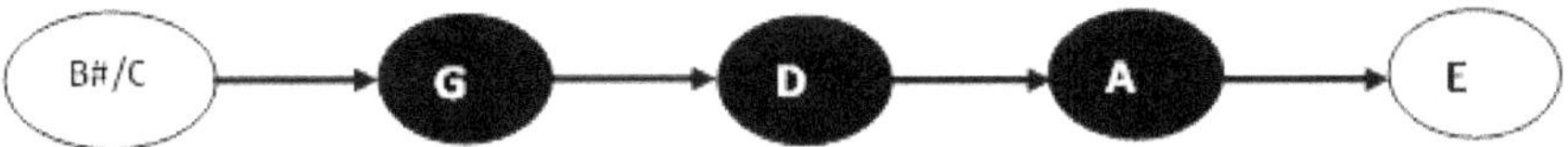

•Now for our last note we will start counting at B# or in other words C and as usual just by looking at our mirror we already have our 1st note B# the root and our last note the 5th G.

•So starting at B# we will go up one letter to the right landing on G.

•This is going up a perfect 5th interval landing on G.

•So now we lower the G by a half step to F#.

•This spells our B# diminished chord as B#D#F#.

VERTICAL RELATIONSHIP BETWEEN NOTES ALONG LINES 1, 2 AND 3.

THE SHARP SIDE (#).

●All the notes vertically along lines 1 and 2 and vice versa starting at f# and G or G and f# all the way to b# and C# or C# and b# are separated by an interval of a half step going up or down respectively.

● All the notes vertically along lines 2 and 3 and vice versa starting at C and a or a and C all the way to C# and a# or a# and C# are separated by a minor 3rd interval or 3 half steps going down or up respectively.

THE FLAT SIDE (♭).

● All the notes vertically along lines 1 and 2 starting at f ♭ and C ♭ all the way to b ♭ and F are separated by a perfect 5th interval going up which is equal to seven half steps or a perfect 4th interval going down which is equal to 5 half steps.

●All the notes vertically along lines 2 and 1 starting at C ♭ and f ♭ all the way to F and b ♭ are separated by a perfect 4th interval going up which is equal to 5 half steps or a perfect 5th interval going down which is equal to seven half steps.

●All the notes vertically along lines 2 and 3 starting at C ♭ and a ♭ all the way to C and a are separated by a minor 3rd interval going down which is equal to 3 half steps.

● All the notes vertically along lines 3 and 2 starting at a ♭ and C ♭ all the way to a and C are separated by a minor 3rd interval going up which is equal to 3 half steps.

CHAPTER 6

<u>FINDING NOTES THAT ARE A WHOLE STEP APART</u>

●You can easily identify notes that are a whole step apart by starting at any note or letter on the mirror and either going up or down two letters.

●The letter or note you land on is a whole step interval away from the note or letter you started on.

●This is actually going up or down in two perfect fifths intervals.

<u>LET US START ON THE SHARP SIDE OF OUR MIRROR</u>

●Let us start at C and go up two letters landing us on D which is a whole step above C.

●This is actually going up in two perfect 5ths intervals.

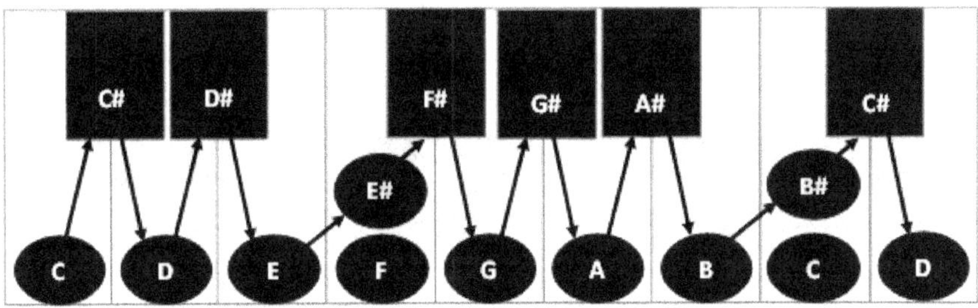

●This is going up in two perfect 5ths intervals.

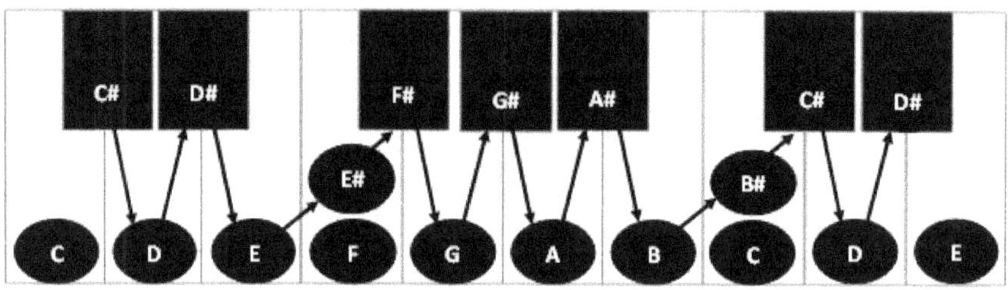

●We will go up two letters landing us on G#.

●This is going up in two perfect 5ths intervals.

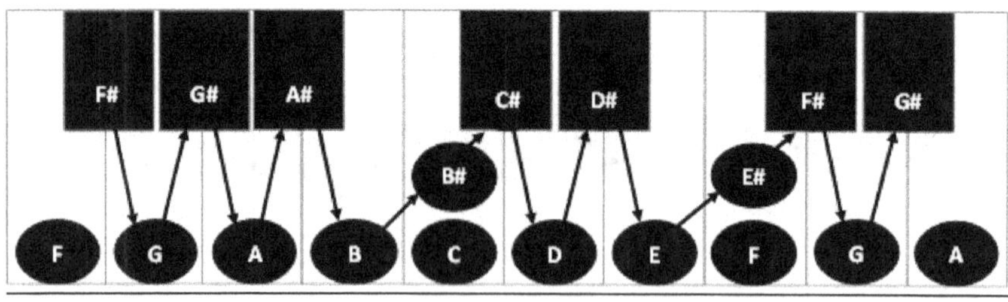

●Let us start at C ♭ along line 1 and go down two letters to the left of C ♭ landing us on A along line 3 on the flat side of our mirror.

●This is actually going down in two perfect 5ths intervals.

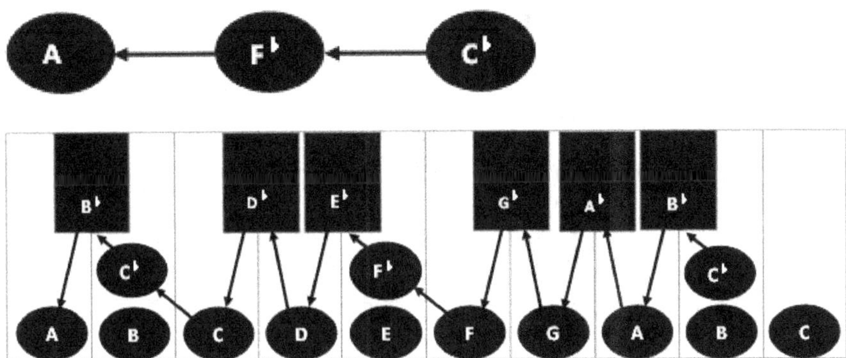

*LET US TRY G ♭ EITHER ON LINE 1 OR 2 AND GO DOWN TWO LETTERS TO THE LEFT OF G ♭ .

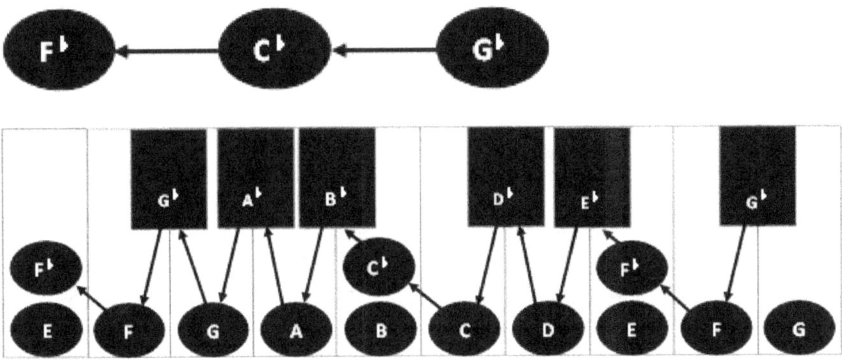

●This is actually going down in two perfect 5ths intervals.

●We go down two letters to the left of A landing on G.

●This is actually going down in two perfect 5ths intervals.

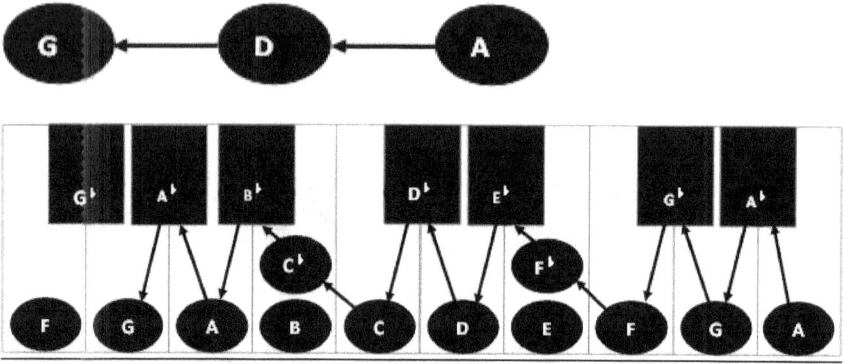

●We go down two letters to the left of A ♭ landing us on G ♭ .

●This is actually going down in two perfect 5ths intervals.

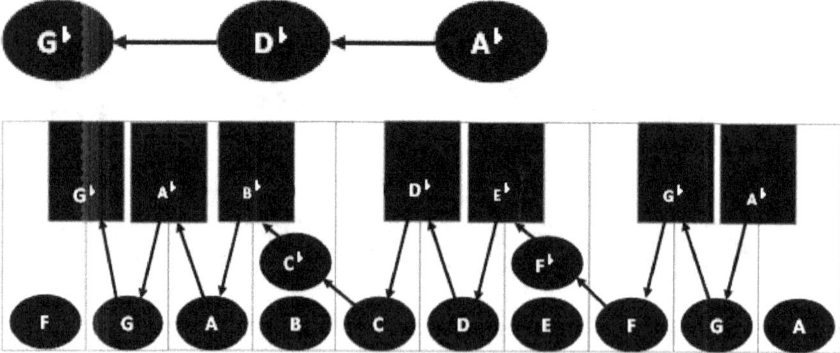

●Now applying the above technique, you can easily create any
whole step scale you would like.

FIGURING OUT THE TRITONE INTERVAL FOR EACH NOTE

THE SHARP (#) SIDE OF THE MIRROR

●Let us start on the sharp side of the mirror.

●A tritone interval is 6 half steps or 6 semitones interval away from a note, also called a diminished 5th interval.

●To figure out a tritone interval between any two notes, we will pick any one note from the mirror.

●For example, C and go up one letter to the right landing us on G we then lower this letter by a half step to G♭/F#.

●Going up one letter to the right of C on our mirror is going up a perfect 5th interval on the keyboard which is equal to 7 half steps from C to G.

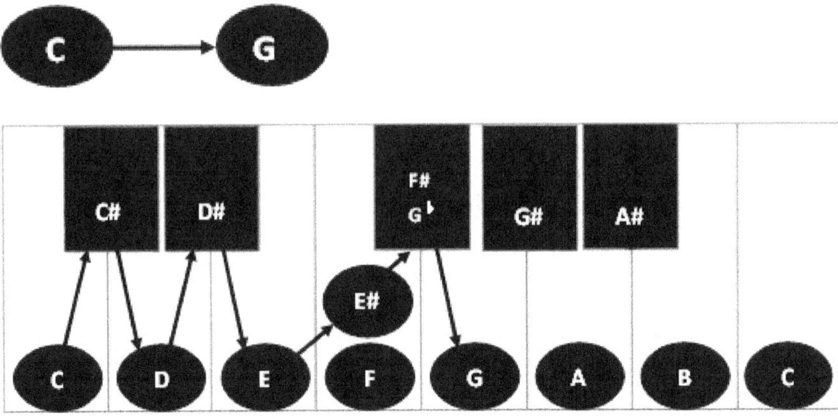

●So the tritone of C is G♭/F#.

●To quickly and easily identify tritone intervals on the sharp side of the mirror we will look at notes along line 2 on the sharp side of the mirror.

•We will pick any note along line 2 and the note that is diagonally to the right above it along line 1 is its tritone interval.

•For example, C and F#, G and C #, D and G#, A and D#, E and A#, B and E# and finally F# and B#.

•Inversely you can pick any note along line 1and the note that is diagonally to the left below it along line 2 is its tritone interval.

•For example F# and C, C# and G, all the way to B# and F#.

*LET US TRY B#.

•We go up one letter to the right of B#/C landing on G and then lowering the G by a half step to G ♭ /F#.

•You may wonder how we got to G when counting up in perfect fifths intervals, but remember B# and C are enharmonic keys and on the keyboard they are one and the same note.

•Going up one letter to the right of B#/C is going up a perfect 5th interval which is equal to 7 half steps from B#/C to G on the keyboard.

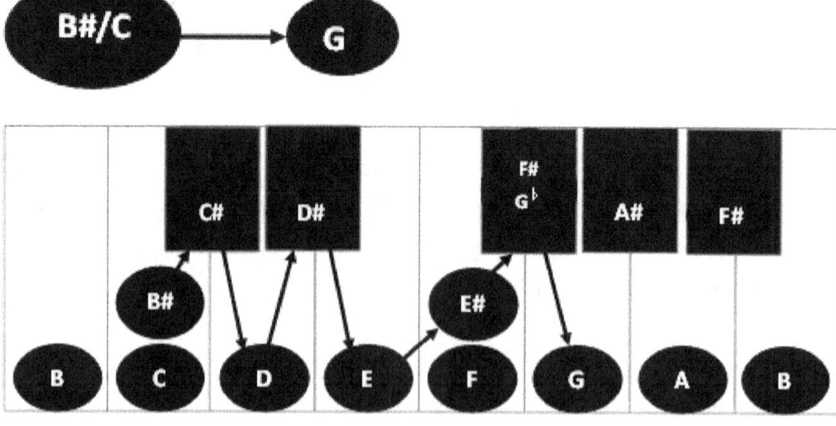

•So the tritone of B# is G ♭ /F#.

•To find the tritone of A# we go up one letter to the right of A# landing on E#.

•Going up one letter to the right of A# is going up a perfect 5th interval which is equal to 7 half steps from A# to E#/F on the keyboard.

•We then lower the E#/F by a half step to E.

•So the tritone of A# is E.

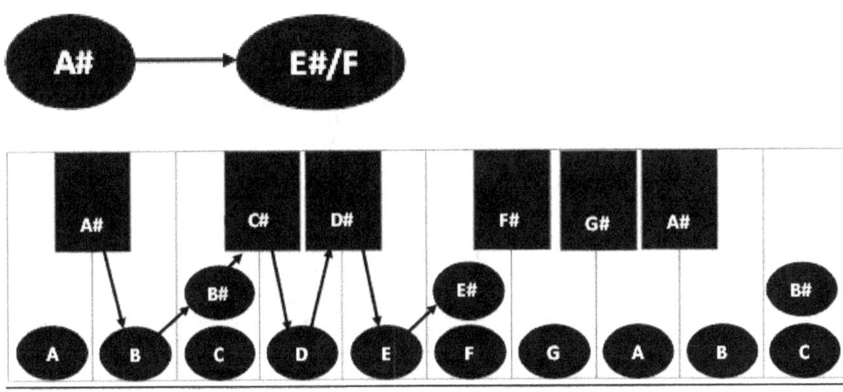

THE FLAT (♭) SIDE OF THE MIRROR

•Now let us go to the flat side of our mirror.

•We take any note say C ♭ and go down one letter to the left landing on F ♭ .

•We then raise the F ♭ by a half step to F.

•So the tritone for C ♭ /B is F.

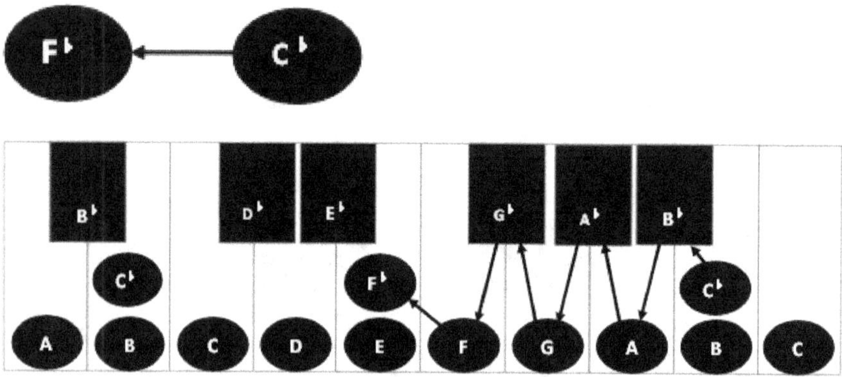

•Going down one letter to the left of C ♭ /B to F ♭ is going down a perfect 5th interval which is equal to 7 half steps from C ♭ to F ♭ on the keyboard.

*LET US TRY A ♭ EITHER ON LINE 1 OR 3.

•We go down one letter to the left of A ♭ landing on D ♭ .

•We then raise D ♭ by a half step to D.

•Going down one letter to the left of A ♭ is going down a perfect 5th interval which is equal to 7 half steps from A ♭ to D ♭ on the keyboard.

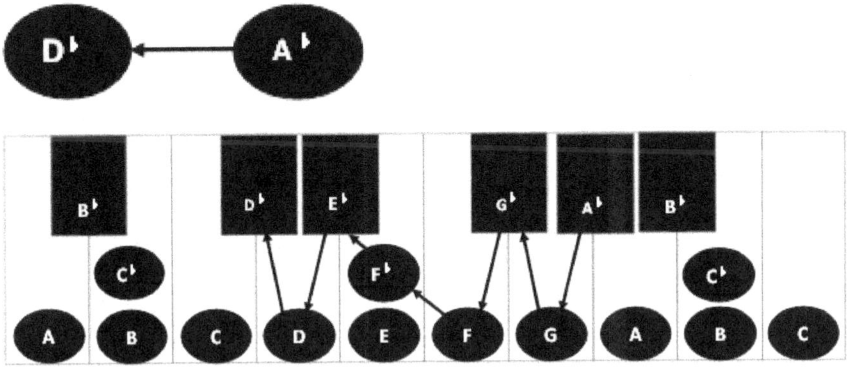

●So the tritone interval for A ♭ is D.

*LET US TRY C EITHER ON LINE 2 OR 3.

●We go down one letter to the left of C landing on F.

●We then raise the F by a half step to F#/G ♭ .

●This is an enharmonic key and since we are on the flat side of the mirror we will call this note G ♭ .

●Going down one letter to the left of C is going down a perfect 5th interval which is equal to 7 half steps from C to F on the keyboard.

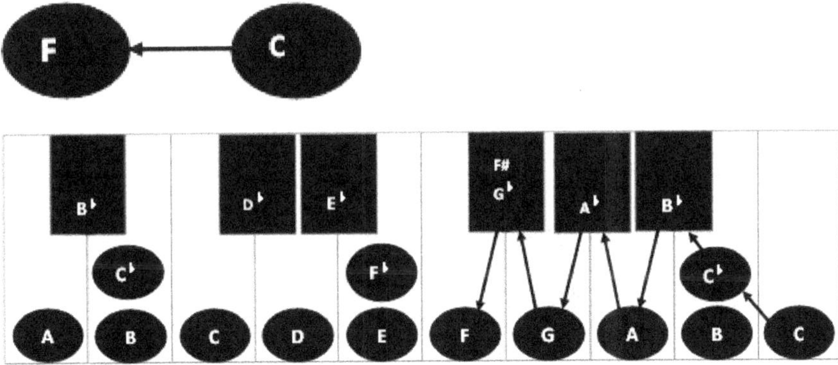

●So, the tritone for C is G ♭ .

●To quickly identify the tritone intervals on the flat side of the mirror we will look at notes along line 2.

●We will pick any note along line 2 on the flat side of the mirror and then raise the note above it along line 1 by a half step.

●Inversely you can pick any note along line 1 on the flat side of the mirror and then lower the note directly below it along line 2 by a half step.

●Let us try C ♭ the note above it is F ♭ .

●We will then raise the F ♭ by a half step to F.

●So, the tritone interval for C ♭ is F.

*LET'S TRY THE LAST TRITONE INTERVAL.

●We will take A along line 3 and go down one letter to the left of A landing us on D.

●We then raise the D by a half step to D#/E ♭ .

●This is an enharmonic key and since we are on the flat side of the mirror we will call this note E ♭ .

●Going down one letter to the left of A to D is going down a perfect 5th interval which is equal to 7 half steps from A to D on the keyboard.

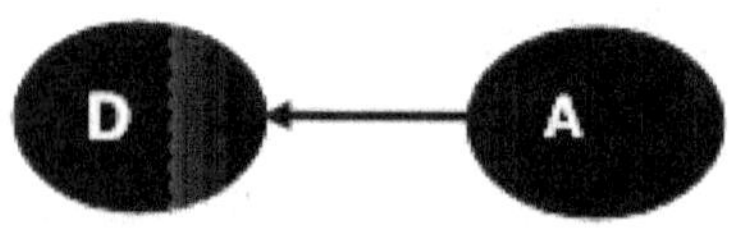

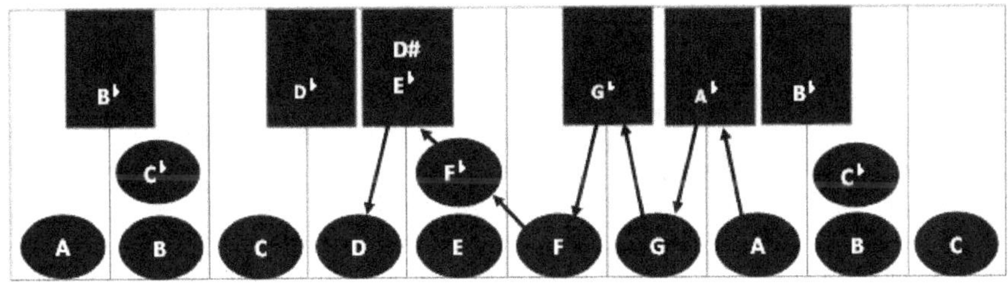

●So, the tritone interval of A is E ♭ .

FINDING OUT THE NOTES OF ANY MAJOR OR MINOR KEY USING THE MIRROR

THE SHARP (#) SIDE

1. LET US SAY WE WANT TO FIND OUT THE NOTES OF THE C MAJOR SCALE.

●Identify where C is along line 2 on our mirror as well as the note below it A.

●We then go down one letter to the left of C and A to find our next pair of notes which are F and D.

●Going down one letter to the left of C and A is actually going down a perfect 5th interval which is equal to 7 half steps on the keyboard for both notes.

●We then go up one letter to the right of C and A counting each pair of notes to get to G and E.

●This is going up a perfect 5th interval which is equal to 7 half steps for the pair of notes.

●Finally, we go up one letter to the right of G and E counting each pair of notes to get to D and B.

●Going up one letter to the right of G and E is actually going up a perfect 5th interval which is equal to 7 half steps on the keyboard from G and E to D and B.

●Now we have the following notes:

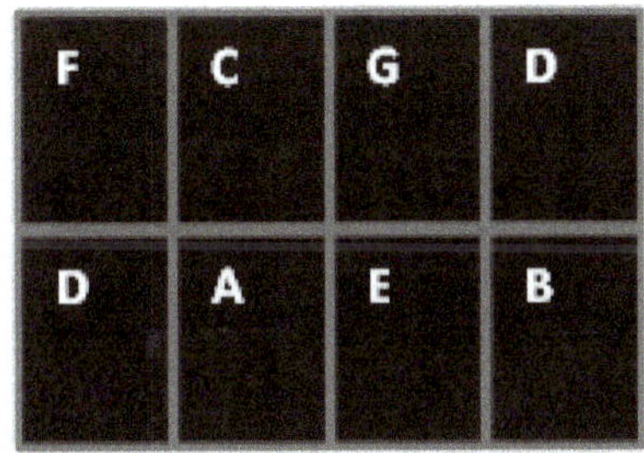

•Here we have 8 random notes with one that is repeated.

•We will cancel the repeated note because in any major or minor key/scale there are only 7 notes.

•We now rearrange the remaining notes in alphabetical order to spell our C major scale as C D E F G A B.

2. LET US SAY WE WANT TO FIND OUT THE NOTES OF THE C# MAJOR SCALE.

•Identify where C# is along line 2 on our mirror as well as the note below it A#.

•We then go down one letter to the left of C# and A# to find our next pair of notes which are F# and D#.

•Going down one letter to the left of C# and A# is actually going down a perfect 5th interval which is equal to 7 half steps on the keyboard for both notes.

•We then go up one letter to the right of C# and A# counting each pair of notes to get to G# and E# along line 1.

•This is going up a perfect 5th interval which is equal to 7 half steps for the pair of notes that is C# and A# respectively.

•Finally, we go up one letter to the right of G# and E# counting each pair of notes to get to D# and B#.

•Going up one letter to the right of G# and E# is actually going up a perfect 5th interval which is equal to 7 half steps on the keyboard from G# and E# to D# and B#.

•And now we have the following notes:

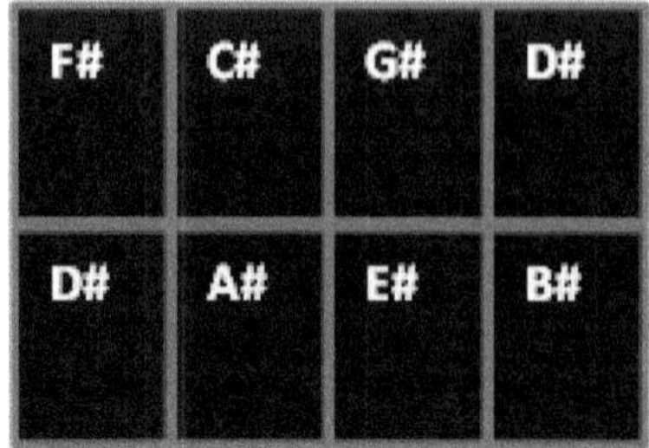

•Here we have 8 random notes with one note that is repeated.

•We will cancel the repeated note because in any major or minor key/scale there are only 7 notes.

•We will now rearrange the following notes in alphabetical order to spell our C# major scale as C# D# E# F# G# A# B#.

3. LET US SAY WE WANT TO FIND OUT THE NOTES OF THE F# MAJOR SCALE.

•Identify where F# is along line 2 on our mirror as well as the note below it D#.

•We then go down one letter to the left of F# and D# to find out our next pair of notes which are B and G#.

•Going down one letter to the left of F# and D# is actually going down a perfect 5th interval which is equal to 7 half steps on the keyboard for both notes respectively.

•We then go up one letter to the right of F# and D# counting each pair of notes to get to C# and A#.

•This is going up a perfect 5th interval which is equal to 7 half steps for the pair of notes that is F# and D# respectively.

•Finally, we go up one letter to the right of C# and A# counting each pair of notes to get to G# and E#.

•Going up one letter to the right of C# and A# is actually going up a perfect 5th interval which is equal to 7 half steps on the keyboard from C# and A# to G# and E# respectively.

•And now we have the following notes:

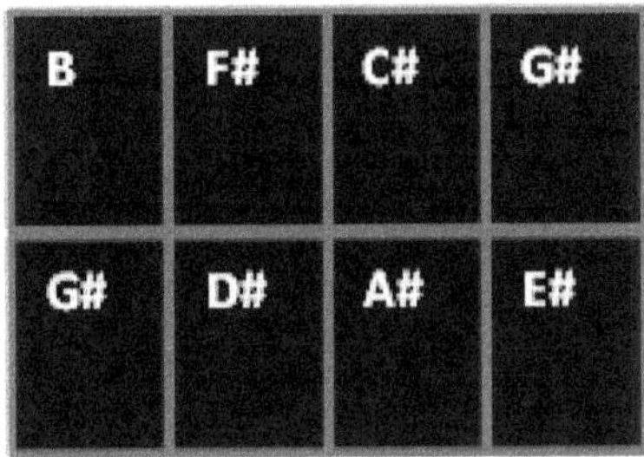

•Here we have 8 random notes with one that is repeated.

•We will cancel the repeated note because in any major or minor key/scale there are only 7 notes.

•We now rearrange the remaining notes in alphabetical order to spell our F# major scale as F# G# A# B C# D# E#.

THE FLAT (♭) SIDE

1. LET US TRY TO CREATE THE C ♭ MAJOR SCALE.

●Identify where C ♭ is along line 2 on our mirror as well as the note below it A ♭ .

●We then go down one letter to the left of C ♭ and A ♭ to find out our next pair of notes which are F ♭ and D ♭ .

●Going down one letter to the left of C ♭ and A ♭ is actually going down a perfect 5th interval which is equal to 7 half steps on the keyboard for both notes.

●We then go up one letter to the right of C ♭ and A ♭ counting each pair of notes to get to G ♭ and E ♭ .

●This is going up a perfect 5th interval which is equal to 7 half steps for the pair of notes that is C ♭ and A ♭ respectively.

●Finally, we go up one letter to the right of G ♭ and E ♭ counting each pair of notes to get to D ♭ and B ♭ .

●Going up one letter to the right of G ♭ and E ♭ is actually going up a perfect 5th interval which is equal to 7 half steps on the keyboard from G ♭ and E ♭ to D ♭ and B ♭ respectively.

●And now we have the following notes:

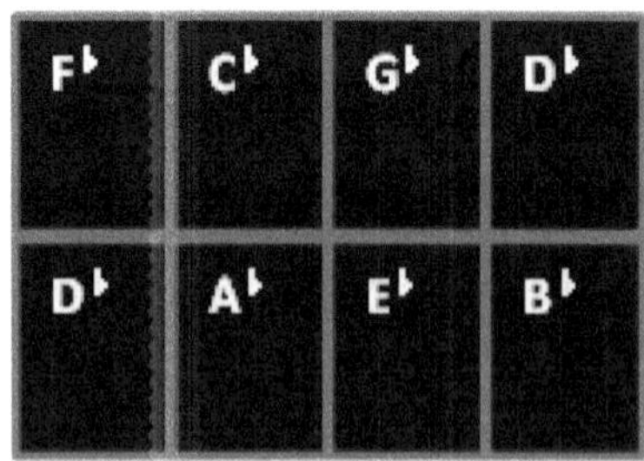

• Here we have 8 random notes with one that is repeated.

• We will cancel the repeated note because in any major or minor key/scale there are only 7 notes.

• We now rearrange the remaining notes in alphabetical order to spell our C ♭ major key or scale as C ♭ D ♭ E ♭ F ♭ G ♭ A ♭ B ♭ .

2. LET US TRY TO CREATE THE F MAJOR KEY.

• Identify where F is along line 2 on our mirror as well as the note below it D

• We then go down one letter to the left of F and D to find our next pair of notes which are B ♭ and G.

• Going down one letter to the left of F and D is actually going down a perfect 5th interval which is equal to 7 half steps on the keyboard for both notes.

• We then go up one letter to the right of F and D counting each pair of notes to get to C and A.

• This is going up a perfect 5th interval which is equal to 7 half steps for the pair of notes that is F and D respectively.

• Finally, we go up one letter to the right of C and A counting each pair of notes to get to G and E.

• Going up one letter to the right of C and A is actually going up a perfect 5th interval which is equal to 7 half steps on the keyboard from C and A to G and E respectively.

• And now we have the following notes:

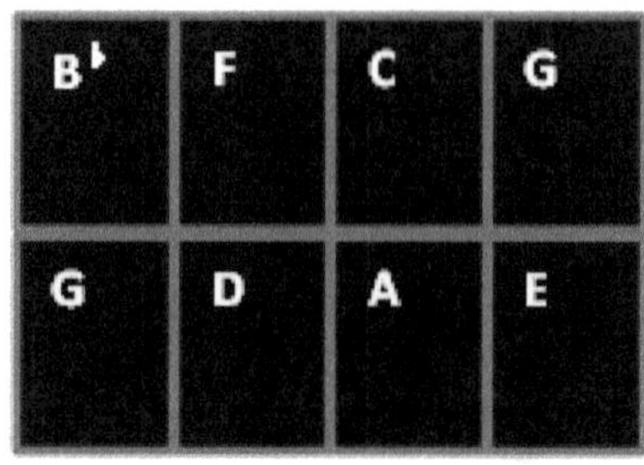

•Here we have 8 random notes with one note that is repeated.

•We will cancel the repeated note because in any major or minor key/scale there are only 7 notes.

•We now rearrange the remaining notes in alphabetical order to spell our F major key/scale as F G A B ♭ C D E.

3. LET US TRY TO CREATE THE G MINOR KEY.

•Identify where G is along line 3 on our mirror as well as the note above it B ♭ .

•We then go down one letter to the left of G and B ♭ to find our next pair of notes which are C and E ♭ .

•Going down one letter to the left of G and B ♭ is actually going down a perfect 5th interval which is equal to 7 half steps on the keyboard for both notes.

•We then go up one letter to the right of G and B ♭ counting each pair of notes to get to D and F.

•This is going up a perfect 5th interval which is equal to 7 half steps on the keyboard for the pair of notes that is G and B ♭ respectively.

•Finally, we go up one letter to the right of D and F counting each pair of notes to get to A and C.

●Going up one letter to the right of D and F is actually going up a perfect 5th interval which is equal to 7 half steps on the keyboard from D and F to A and C respectively.

●And now we have the following notes:

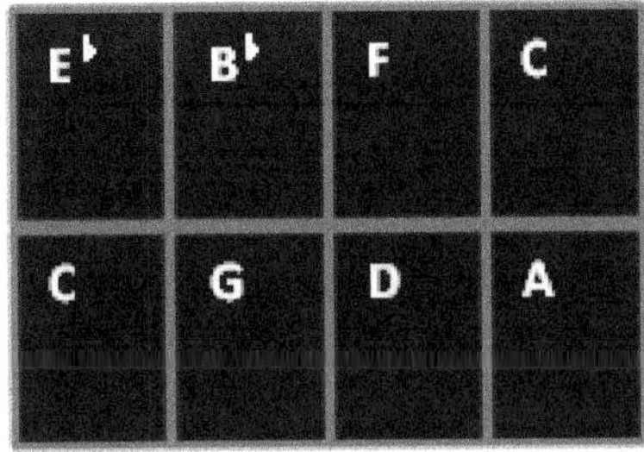

●Here we have 8 random notes with one note that is repeated.

●We will cancel the repeated note because in any major or minor key/scale there are only 7 notes.

●We now rearrange the remaining notes in alphabetical order to spell our G minor key/scale as G A B ♭ C D E ♭ F.